IDEA-LINKS

the

new

creativity

.

IDEA-LINKS

the

new

creativity

JIM LINK

BEAVER'S
POND
PRESS

ISBN 13: 978-1-59298-275-2

Library of Congress Catalog Number: 2012900501

Printed in the United States of America

First Printing: 2012

16 15 14 13 12   5 4 3 2 1

Cover and interior design by James Monroe Design, LLC.

BEAVER'S
POND
PRESS

Beaver's Pond Press
7108 Ohms Lane
Edina, MN 55439–2129
952-829-8818
www.BeaversPondPress.com

To order, visit www.BeaversPondBooks.com
or call 1-800-901-3480. Reseller discounts available.
For more information, visit **TheNewCreativity.com**

To all . . .

creative people who feel misunderstood.

"noncreative" people who've been misdiagnosed or given the wrong prescription.

leaders and managers who are struggling to make their teams more creative.

I hope this helps.

Table of Contents

Part Two: Creative Reframing

Part Three: Planning for Success

Introduction

Can You *Really* Become More Creative?

What if I told you that much of what you've heard about creativity has sent you down the wrong path? That getting to the "Eureka!" or "Aha!" moment you've been searching for isn't the result of fun, or play, or some magical unleashing. Instead, it's the result of two simple disciplines that creative people have followed most of their lives. And what if I told you I could teach you and your team how to become more creative by following these two simple disciplines? Would you think it's possible? If you're skeptical, I understand.

Say Goodbye to Wacky

When I speak to corporate audiences, I often ask people to rate how much they think their creativity has improved over the last five, ten, or fifteen years. Most admit to no gain. A small number think they've gotten a little better—an equal number, a little worse. Some believe their organizations have become more innovative, but not because of any increase in their personal creativity. It's not for lack of trying. Companies and individuals spend billions of dollars each year on creativity books, creativity training, and motivational speakers, but a 2010 *Newsweek* cover story concluded we're actually much less creative than twenty years ago.[1] So what gives? Why aren't all the books and training and speakers making us more creative?

The most common creativity books contain exhaustive lists of creative exercises, all recycling similar approaches and calling them something different. If you picked up this book hoping you or your team could become more creative, there's a good chance you own a few creative exercise books as well. I own a bunch. Here's the problem with creative exercise books: The exercises will work, but people rarely use them. I know the exercises in these books can work because I use variations of them when I run my own ideation sessions. I know they're rarely used, because the people I work with tell me so. Unless you're a professional ideation moderator, there are too many exercises and never enough time to find the right one for the problem at hand. So the exercise books adorn bookshelves, gather dust, and create the illusion of greater personal creativity.

The other shortcoming of creative exercise books is that they don't actually make you a more creative person. They are to creativity what joke books are to humor. If you recite a joke from a joke book and people laugh, you're funny at that moment. But you aren't any funnier as a person. Creativity exercises are like that—if you manage to find the right exercise and use it properly, it may help you create an idea. But it won't make you any more creative as a person, once the book is back on the shelf.

Beyond the creative exercise books are speakers and seminars, many of which are very energizing and fun. Some teach you to use improvisational humor; others advise you to suppress your inner critic, or forgive your third-grade teacher for laughing at your science-fair project. "Be playful and wacky and the ideas will come," some say.

I don't want to sound harsh; some creativity books and seminars serve an important role. Without question, innovation improves when you're more open to other people's ideas and less critical of your own. And who can argue with having fun? On the other hand, are you more creative than you were before the workshop, before you wore that silly hat . . . ? My informal poll of those who attend these learn-to-be-more-playful seminars would suggest the answer is no. Acting goofy and tossing toys around a room only succeeds in moving toys from one place to another. The needle on your creativity meter remains static. It's time to kiss wackiness good-bye.

How Ideas Really Happen

Twenty-five years spent generating ideas and helping others generate them across hundreds of product and service categories has opened my eyes to how ideas really happen. On the surface, the process seems impossibly random, as if an idea is mysteriously channeled to its inventor like a thunderbolt from above—the fabled eureka moment. Yet, it seems, many ideas come from the same people, over and over again. But what's under the surface? Is there something we're not seeing? What gives these "idea people" the apparent ability to generate ideas at will? And, if eureka moments are serendipitous, why do some people experience more of them than others? More importantly, if we uncover whatever it is they're doing differently, can "it" be taught to others? Is it possible for someone to become more creative?

One theory posits that some people just have it and others don't. Another is that everyone's blessed with innate creative ability that's just waiting to be unleashed. I say it's something else altogether.

I tackled this mystery in 2007, when I agreed to prepare a speech on the topic, "How Can I Become a More Creative Person?" even though I wasn't entirely sure of the answer. At one point, uncomfortable with the prospect of leading my audience through a bunch of creative exercises I knew they wouldn't use, I nearly gave up, ready to fall back on the old some-people-have-it-and-some-people-don't explanation. While the statement is partially true, the fear of giving an eight-word speech motivated me to dig deeper, to really think about the creative people I've worked with the past twenty-five years, and to figure out what they're doing differently.

Here's the great news: It didn't turn into an eight-word speech, and nobody had to memorize fifty exercises. I've cracked a critical piece of creative code and I will show you—as I've shown others since that speech—how you can increase your current level of creativity. But first, you'll need to let go of the notion that creative ability is an innate skill, latent in all of us, and just waiting to be unleashed through goofy play or driving to work a new way. Second, you'll need to accept that waiting around for standing-in-the-shower eureka moments to occur isn't a viable strategy either. If it were, every office, cube, and conference room would sport a working showerhead. Instead, you'll need to acquire creativity in the same ordinary way you'd develop any other skill: By learning and applying specific disciplines consistently over time.

When it comes to being creative, there is no free lunch. You can't and won't become more creative overnight, and if someone tells you otherwise, cover your wallet or purse. But I promise that the disciplines you'll learn aren't as painful as they sound. With time and practice, you'll become proficient and the whole process will become second nature. Maybe even fun.

No, there's no magical unleashing. And what a relief! You don't have to endure another kooky workshop; you don't have to wait for a thunderbolt; you just have to put in the work. If you're truly committed to becoming more creative or to increasing the collective creativity of your team or company, I welcome you to the rest of the book. Yes, you really can become more creative.

Visual Overview of the Book

For all you visual thinkers, here's a handy framework instead of a table of contents. Parts one and two explain and teach you the two important disciplines you'll need to become more creative. Part three incorporates these disciplines into a plan so you can more effectively utilize them as a team or throughout your organization.

Along the way, you're going to adopt new behaviors and acquire new tools and techniques that will help you burn these two new disciplines into your everyday thinking. Put them all together and the book looks like this:

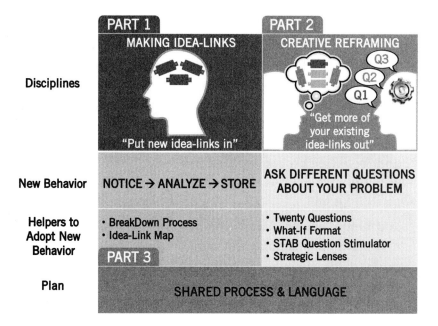

While the visual rendering won't make sense at first, as you progress it will help you see how all the pieces fit together and relate to each other, and serve as a "you are here" marker as you navigate the book.

We begin our journey by rethinking creativity and seeing how the allure of the fabled eureka moment actually distracts us from focusing on the important work that leads us there.

1

Shattering the Eureka Illusion

Think about the most creative person you work with. What do you suppose makes him or her so creative in the first place?

Ask employees at the Toro Company's world headquarters, "Who's highly creative here?" and odds are one of the names you'll hear is Jack Gust. Jack doesn't look like your typical "creative." He dresses pretty much like the other engineers. He doesn't sport a soul patch or wear funky glasses. His cube looks like any other cube. There's no barber chair, purple carpet, or any of the contrived trappings that usually label someone as "creative." He attends all the same meetings as the other engineers, and with the exception of his highly developed ability to good-naturedly trash-talk fellow employees, Jack blends in with everyone else.

Yet, Jack Gust's long list of creative achievements at Toro sets him apart. So what's he doing differently? Ask him and he'll gladly tell you some of his creative triggers. Then he'll pull out his ace in the hole, the aptly labeled "File of Interesting Things." As part of his daily life—at work and at home—Jack is hyper alert for new products, new features, and new ways of doing things both within his industry—golf-course maintenance equipment—and outside it. Sometimes he's tuned into stuff *way* outside of his industry.

"If I go to a trade show, or see an interesting new product feature in a magazine, I put it in my file and take mental note of what the feature or idea is all about—what makes it interesting in the first place, what makes it work. In some rare cases, it leads to an immediate idea, but most times, I just file it away and sure enough one of them seems to magically pop up when I'm trying to solve a creative problem."[2]

I watch Jack as he thumbs through his stack, occasionally pausing on a particular clipping to tell me how it eventually connected to a new product success. As he reaches the end, Jack sets down his File of Interesting Things and pauses to summarize the source of his creative luck: "Mostly I'm just really good at paying attention to things."

• • •

Far from the world of turf equipment engineering is singer-songwriter Paul Simon. One of America's most respected songwriters and musicians, Simon was the first recipient of the Library of Congress Gershwin Prize for Popular Song in 2007, honoring the profound and positive effect he's had on popular music. His catalog of work spans more genres than perhaps any other musician, and his ability to create new and relevant music continues into his sixties. In short, Paul Simon may be the most prolific and influential songwriter of the past fifty years. He's a creative genius by nearly anyone's definition.

Surely, Paul Simon was born a creative genius. Or is that only part of the answer? If you listen to Simon explain his songwriting process you'll notice a method that goes beyond his gene pool. You see, Simon has his own file of interesting things, but in his case the "files" are in his head and the "things" are sounds. For as long as he can remember, Simon has made meticulous mental notes of music and sounds that caught his attention. Not the entire song, but the *pieces*—a chord sequence here, a drumbeat there, a smooth blending of harmonies.

"Something about the way I heard was sort of cataloging and remembering sounds and combinations of sounds. I can remember thinking, 'I like this record because I like the sound of the drum.' So, even though my attention as a singer was as a duo, I was paying attention to a lot of other stuff about pop music of the time. Those sounds I've kept straight through my whole career."[3]

These musical pieces Simon notices, analyzes, and catalogs are what "works" in some manner to generate interest or create a feeling, even if only for a second. Some of the pieces Simon returns to again and again. The *who-bop-a-loo-chi-bop*-type harmony of The Everly Brothers, one of Simon's earliest inspirations, shows up repeatedly, in songs as diverse as 1968's "Mrs. Robinson" (*koo-koo-ka-choo*) to 1985's "Diamonds on the Soles of Her Shoes" (*ah-waka-waka-wak*).[4]

As he's writing music, seemingly out of the blue, short sounds, rhythms, or sequences link together to form the basis for a song or to help him solve a portion of it. Pieces of interesting things—the musical elements extracted from Simon's past—lead to timeless, original music.

• • •

Let's take one more unexpected turn, this time far from the world of, well, this world. Meet Stefani Joanne Angelina Germanotta, better known as the Grammy- and MTV Award–winning entertainer Lady Gaga. While Gaga's appeal is a matter of personal taste, there's no arguing her incredible success as a creative musical artist and an influential force in the world of glam and fashion. Surely someone as flamboyantly creative as Lady Gaga is simply a free spirit whose creativity naturally oozes from her very being. Though perhaps *oozes* is too gentle a term for Gaga, who described the creative process for her release *Born This Way* as "15 minutes of gigantic regurgitation of thoughts and feelings."[5]

While Gaga may vomit ideas, to truly grasp her creativity, we need to understand not how her ideas get out, but rather how they get in. As she explains *the source* of her creativity, it's anything but flamboyant and controversial. In fact, you might even call Lady Gaga boring. Studious. She calls herself a "librarian" of pop culture.[6] In reality, she's more of a historian.

"I myself can look at almost any hemline, silhouette, beadwork or heel architecture and tell you very precisely who designed it after them, and what cultural and musical movement parented the birth, death and resurrection of that particular trend," she boasts. "An expertise in the vocabulary of fashion, art and pop culture requires a tremendous amount of studying."[7]

So what exactly does she study? Lady Gaga keeps a keen eye on the world around her, analyzing "everything from vintage books and magazines I found at the Strand on 12th Street to my dad's old Bowie posters to metal records from my best friend Lady Starlight to Aunt Merle's hand-me-down emerald-green designer pumps."[8] Gaga calls the product of her careful study her "library cards," as in the reference cards once used in libraries. She files these reference cards away in her brain, mixes them up in new and different ways, then regurgitates them as award-winning songs, videos, and fashions.

Lady Gaga studying? Library cards? What's going on here?

Rethinking Creativity

When we think about creativity, we naturally think of the moment an idea is born—the eureka moment, the flash of genius, a thunderbolt from the blue, or channeling some mysterious force. It's the stuff of movies and inventor lore. So energizing, so celebrated, and so romantic is the eureka moment that we find ourselves hyper-focused on trying to recreate the circumstances around it. Because the moment feels so free and natural, we've landed on the illusion that creativity is an innate skill, just waiting to be unleashed, if only someone could help us become as free and playful as the moment itself. This has led us all down the wrong path.

We'd never consider attending a one-day seminar called "Unleash Your Ability to Organize," nor would we sign up for "Unleash Your Ability to Bench Press 400 Pounds" or "Unleash Your Ability to Fly a Helicopter." The idea that these skills could be "unleashed" in a single day is ludicrous. Yet, many eagerly shell out good money to send their team to a seminar called "Unleash Your Creative Potential." The wonder and mystery of the eureka moment supports the romantic notion that simply by removing internal barriers or "having fun," we can increase the frequency of these moments in our own lives. Unfortunately, when we focus on the moment of invention and wait for the unleashing, we ignore the boring, mundane part that sets up the moment, and thus, we miss the real lesson toward becoming more creative. It's not the visible part of idea generation you want to emulate. It's the part you don't see—the foundation that allows the moment to happen. The ninety percent of the iceberg that isn't visible contains the real reason some people are idea-generation machines and some aren't.

Making the Unconscious Conscious

So what exactly are creative people like Jack Gust, Paul Simon, and Lady Gaga doing differently? When I started down this path, I figured I was probably the ten-thousandth person to ask the same question: Why are some people more creative than others? I knew if I found the answer, it would probably be painfully simple in hindsight (it was), and if I found a new answer, it would come from asking a different question (it did).

To conduct my quest, I relied on the power of analogy. I asked myself, "Is there another skill (and make no mistake, creativity is a skill) in which some are naturally gifted and some are, by nature, more challenged? More importantly, is there a skill in which those who first consider themselves deficient can ultimately prevail and noticeably improve their ability?" After some consideration, I found the perfect analogous skill that could unlock the secret to becoming more creative: Organization.

Let me start by saying my brain isn't naturally wired toward organization, but I've always dreamed of becoming an organized person. In Myers-Briggs parlance, you could say I have J-envy. So one day, out of both curiosity and envy, I asked one of my über-organized friends (you know—the kind with *no* loose papers, only color-coded folders neatly staggered in an upright holder), "How do you keep your life so organized and get your work done at the same time?"

After a bit of hesitation, during which she was no doubt calculating whether such a hopeless case was worth her effort, she shared a very simple principle: "a place for everything and everything in its place." As a somewhat impulsive creative person, this shocked me. "So let me get this right," I asked, "you actually take the time to think about where things should go and create a space for it, as opposed to adding it to a stack or stuffing it in a drawer while promising to get to it later?"

"Yep," she said, "every time. Right away, if possible. Doesn't everybody?"

Well, frankly, no, but I must admit the idea of no stacks intrigued me. Like many "stackers," I believed that the only solution to my Grand Teton–rivaling piles of clutter was arson. I was motivated to try something to improve my ability to organize my surroundings, and the place-for-everything, everything-in-its-place discipline seemed simple enough. As I gradually (and sometimes grudgingly) applied the place-for-everything principle, my environment slowly transformed. Office keys could be found on a hook labeled "Office Keys" instead of under a popcorn bag. Flannel shirts, crew necks, and dress shirts each formed their own affinity group in my closet, no longer randomly strewn across ten feet of wooden dowel. Morning shirt selection was now a snap. I even thought about labeling my home label maker "Home Label Maker" but was already on shaky ground with my wife after labeling several basement boxes "Janet's Junk."

One day I realized that I had sought to become more organized and had actually achieved it! How did it happen? I adopted a simple discipline that makes naturally organized people organized: Take a small amount of time to create a place for the thing, then put the damned thing in it. All past attempts to instill order had failed, but keeping it simple and following that one easy-to-understand discipline worked. After ten years of steady application, I can report with great confidence and pride that I am, at long last, an organized person.

So what does that have to do with creativity? What's the conclusion we can draw? If you ask highly organized people why they're organized, most will simply say, "I just am." They've been organized since they were kids and become more organized as they get older. Sure, if you really analyze it, they follow certain principles. But it's largely unintentional or unconscious; they naturally do the things that result in a more organized environment, such as creating a place for everything and putting things in their places. For them the discipline is second nature, but for those of us who struggle with organization, it's a foreign discipline.

The same logic applies with creative people. If you ask highly creative people why they're creative, they'll usually have the same response most organized people do about their organizational skills: "I just am." They didn't seek to become more creative and most haven't really thought about how they do it; creativity just seems to happen for them.

So let's move forward with the following premises:

Organization: The only way less-organized people become more organized is by finding and consciously following simple-to-understand disciplines that highly-organized people do naturally or unconsciously. The more diligently you follow these disciplines, the more organized you become.

Creativity: The only way less-creative people become more creative is by finding and consciously following simple-to-understand disciplines that highly-creative people do naturally or unconsciously. The more diligently you follow these disciplines, the more creative you become.

There are two key points to remember before we proceed. First, you may not have been born with the same characteristics as a highly creative person, but you can consciously and intentionally emulate what highly creative people do naturally. Second, how much you improve your skill is wholly dependent on you. Creativity isn't an all-or-nothing skill. There are degrees of creativity, just as there are degrees of organization, or any skill for that matter. You can go whole hog like I did, and make your office look like an Ikea showroom, or you can go part of the way and become a bit more organized. The point is this: When you control the discipline, you control how much you improve.

This invites the ultimate question: Is there a simple-in-hindsight process that creative people use that makes them so creative? Is there a natural, under-the-surface discipline that people like Jack Gust, Paul Simon, Lady Gaga, and others follow? And once you identify it, can anyone adopt this simple discipline and become a more creative person? After many years of working with and studying ideas and idea-people, I assure you the answer is yes.

The Old Creativity

Creativity is all about
the eureka moment.

Creativity is innate—
it only requires unleashing.

Someone can make you
creative in a four-hour seminar.

The New Creativity

Creativity is all about setting up
the eureka moment.

Creativity is a skill that's
built systematically like any
other skill.

You choose to make yourself
more creative over time.

Part One

Making
Idea-Links

Discipline 1

Making Idea-Links

Creativity isn't a latent ability to be magically unleashed; it's a skill that's improved like any other skill, by learning and then steadily applying the right disciplines.

The first of these disciplines is to make *idea-links*—the "things" you connect to your problem to come up with new ideas. You can think of idea-links as subatomic, idea-making elements that before now were invisible, but have always been there, responsible for the seemingly random aha moments that the old view of creativity attributed to serendipity. Once you see these creative moments at their idea-link level, they'll no longer seem so random.

In learning about how (and why) to make idea-links, you'll suddenly see how you or *anyone* in your organization can truly become more creative.

SIDETRACK:
I'm Not the Fun Police

Before you conclude I'm here to snuff out all the fun in your life, let me be clear: I'm not against having fun on the job. Nor am I against creating an environment that's more conducive to creativity. In fact, I'm decidedly pro-fun and pro-creative environment. It's just that these shiny objects divert our attention from the part of creativity that you can control and that makes the biggest difference—the work part.

There's no seminal moment when the concept of creativity first became synonymous with fun, but it's regularly reinforced in pop culture. Movies like *Big* depict a playful, childlike Tom Hanks running creative circles around his stiff coworkers. Television programs portray comedy writers laughing hysterically as they develop this week's script. And this connection between fun and creativity is reinforced in our own experience. Our eureka moments often arrive with tremendous joy and happiness. It's a short leap to conclude that if the moment of creation is fun, then maybe if I have more fun, I'll have more eureka moments. It's a little like saying: if a clean house makes me feel relaxed, then maybe if I relax more often, it will make my house cleaner. Just because the powerful feeling accompanies the moment, doesn't mean it's responsible for the moment.

The recent fad of tying playfulness to creativity has resulted in a phenomenon author Gordon MacKenzie calls "mandatory fun." Most of us cringe at the games and activities contrived to force-feed fun in the workplace. When we hear the order, "Okay everybody, for the next fifteen minutes we're going to have fun," we don't feel creative. We feel violated. The truth is, you can't mandate fun. But as you'll read later in the book, you can mandate creativity . . . once you know which behaviors to mandate.

Environment is a slightly different matter than fun. Creating an environment conducive to creativity encourages creative behavior and results in more ideas and happier employees. That cause and effect is undeniable. I wholeheartedly support making your environment as idea-friendly as possible. But we need to mentally separate that which encourages creativity from that which builds creativity. For example, if you want to become a better guitar player, constructing a beautiful new studio and surrounding yourself with supportive listeners will encourage and inspire you to play guitar more often and take more risks. But you'll still need to practice scales and improve your skills. You'll need to learn new chords, finger-picking styles, and strumming patterns. These are the disciplines of guitar playing. So the improved environment helps, but it's the learning and regular practice of the disciplines that builds your skills.

I'm not here to take away your fun, or discount the importance of an environment that encourages creativity. I want you to have both. But I also want you to understand the limitations of each. I'm here to focus you on the part of the get-more-creative formula that matters most: the disciplines.

2

Idea-Links: Creativity's Missing Link

Creativity is nothing more than connecting things.
—STEVE JOBS, COFOUNDER OF APPLE

An idea is nothing more or less than a new combination of old elements.
—VILFREDO PARETO, ITALIAN ECONOMIST

As we begin to understand the discipline that creative people follow, consider two of my favorite quotes—one old, one new. Jobs's assertion that creativity is about making connections is a relatively recent statement, but not a new thought. Many books exist about the power of connection-making, including *The Medici Effect: Breakthrough Insights at the Intersection of Ideas, Concepts and Cultures,* Frans Johansson's tale of connections made by the great thinkers who gathered in Florence to usher in the Renaissance.[9] But simply knowing that making connections or "connecting things" is the ultimate goal of creativity is a little like knowing that "doing things" that put the ball in the net is the ultimate goal of soccer. Until we know what the things are, we're not going to score. Likewise, to get better at creativity, we need to know more than "creativity is about making connections." We need to learn what "things" to connect and how to find these "things" in the first place.

The key word in Jobs's quote isn't *connecting*, but rather *things*. That Jobs calls them *things* suggests that until now, whatever people are using to make connections is undefined. The second quote moves us ever so slightly closer toward understanding what these *things* really are.

By saying that ideas come from combining *old* elements, Pareto tells us these *things* come from somewhere in our past. But Pareto's quote still leaves us wondering where they came from and how they were created. Before I answer this, we need to provide these *things* a more worthy and descriptive name. What if we gave Jobs's *things* and Pareto's *old elements* a name that spoke specifically to their ability to create ideas? What if we rewrote Pareto: An idea is nothing more or less than a new combination of old idea-links. One word changed, but the meaning remains the same. Creativity—the act of idea generation—is about connecting old elements to new problems, or as I call these elements, *idea-links*.

Idea-link is a term I've coined to give Pareto's old elements a certain shape and function in your mind, and to highlight their potential to make ideas or connections that link forward and back. These elements, these idea-links, are the *things* that get linked when connections are made.

Stated another way, you can't make connections or linkages unless you have idea-links to draw from.

Using the term *idea-link* will give you and your team a shared vocabulary as you discuss creativity and figure out how to become more creative. No more meetings where one person thinks creativity is about painting the walls purple and another thinks it means having spiky hair. I will soon prove to you that one of two main ways to increase your creativity is to learn to create idea-links, so get ready to add it to your lexicon, and your company's.

Creative Minds Are Made, Not Born

To accept the concept of idea-links, we need to kill the old notion that ideas magically spring forth from mysteriously gifted minds or from lucky people who happen to be in the right place at the right time. True, ideas sometimes happen at the most unexpected times and from the most unusual circumstances, but waiting and hoping for serendipitous moments won't work. The truth is, nearly all ideas need raw material to connect and idea-links are a big part of that raw material. As you'll soon see, manufacturing idea-links is how creative people make their minds more creative.

Just as organized people naturally and instinctively create a place for everything, creative people naturally and instinctively create lots of idea-links. Then, they continually draw from their vast idea-link reserves to generate a seemingly endless stream of ideas. Notice I used the word "naturally." As I've discovered, most creative people go about the process of making idea-links without much fanfare. Many are unaware they're doing it at all. In fact, when I speak to groups and explain the idea-link-making process, invariably the more creative ones in the audience often say, "You're right, I *do* do that. I just figured everybody did." Sounds a lot like our organized friends, doesn't it?

It's time to learn how to make these idea-link deposits for yourself and see how they improve your ability to generate ideas. And then, just like I did at the end of my organization story, you'll make your own proclamation: I *can* become a more creative person!

Making Idea-Links 101

What exactly are idea-links and how do you make them? Here's a definition and a visual representation to get us started:

noun

a succinct **insight or realization**

about **why or how something works** or succeeds

that is **stored into memory.**

As we dig into three different examples, this definition will soon make perfect sense.

Thinking differently

Many of you will be familiar with Steve Jobs's commencement address at Stanford in 2005, "Stay Hungry. Stay Foolish." Within it lies a perfect demonstration of the creation and application of idea-links:

> Reed College at that time offered perhaps the best calligraphy instruction in the country. Throughout the campus every poster, every label on every drawer, was beautifully hand-calligraphied. Because I had dropped out and didn't have to take the normal classes, I decided to take a calligraphy class to learn how to do this. I learned about serif and san serif typefaces, about varying the amount of space between different letter combinations, about what makes great typography great. It was beautiful, historical, artistically subtle in a way that science can't capture, and I found it fascinating.

> None of this had even a hope of any practical application in my life. But ten years later, when we were designing the first Macintosh computer, it all came back to me. And we designed it all into the Mac. It was the first computer with beautiful typography. If I had never dropped in on that single course in college, the Mac would have never had multiple typefaces or proportionally spaced fonts. And since Windows just copied the Mac, it's likely that no personal computer would have them.

Some read this story or watch the video and come to the wrong conclusion: To become more creative I need to be free, do foolish things, or follow my passion. Lost in the passage is one of the true lessons about creativity: What Jobs did to make himself more creative was to think deeply and analytically about calligraphy. Over the years, thousands of people have taken calligraphy courses. But probably few have thought as deeply about "what makes great typography great" as Jobs did. Fewer still filed those thoughts away, despite having no expectation of any practical application later in life.

If you learn how to do calligraphy, you possess a skill. If you know calligraphy finds its origins in multiple cultures, you know a fact. If you realize that proportional spacing is one of the reasons calligraphy looks beautiful, you own an idea-link.

Now let's return to our definition of an idea-link. Proportional spacing and proportional character size is an insight into what makes calligraphy work or succeed. This realization is stored into Jobs's memory. Ten years later, he connects it to a different problem. Each of these is a part of our definition.

If you know calligraphy finds its origins in multiple cultures, you know a fact. If you realize that proportional spacing is one of the reasons calligraphy looks beautiful, you own an idea-link.

When Jobs added the capability for proportional typeface spacing and sizing into his Mac requirements, he made visually interesting fonts possible for a device that up until then had suffered from drab, NASA-like, monospace fonts. The proportional spacing idea-link unleashed a world of fonts that continues to make our techno-gadgets visually appealing and make the joy of design available to all.

Jobs's story also demonstrates three important characteristics of idea-links. First, idea-links are additive. When Steve Jobs takes the idea-link that he pulled from the world of calligraphy and reapplies it to computer design, we say he is creative. If Steve Jobs pulls lots of idea-links from many life experiences and frequently reapplies them elsewhere, we say he is *highly* creative. The same is true for you and me. The more idea-links we own, the more creative potential we possess.

Second, idea-links come with a backstory. Think about your really creative friends or colleagues. Do they often preface their ideas with phrases like "That reminds me of the time . . ." or "That's kind of like . . ."? It seems they can't share their idea without giving you the backstory or analogy first. They aren't trying to annoy you; they are simply drawing on an idea-link from a similar or analogous circumstance to the problem they're trying to solve. (If you married someone like this, you know exactly what I mean.) Anytime you hear someone explain an idea with a backstory, as Jobs did at Stanford, you know there's an idea-link in there, somewhere.

Idea-links are links in a chain. They connect back to the story or example they were extracted from, and connect forward to their new usage—your problem.

Finally, idea-links don't come with a use-by date or a fuse. Jobs never expected to use his knowledge of calligraphy for any useful purpose. But ten years later, he did, in a way that has transformed the lives of millions. Idea-links are like that. If you make an idea-link, you might use it in ten minutes. You might use it in ten days. You might use it in ten years, as Jobs did. You might use it multiple times. There's also a chance you may never use it.

Finding idea-links at home

For the second example, we'll move from other people's lives to your life. If you're on Facebook, you likely fall into one of two categories: People who play Farmville or people who wonder why other people play Farmville. Among those who wonder why other people play Farmville, there is another split: Those who continue to wonder and those who are curious and motivated enough to actually find out why.

First, here's a little background in case you're unfamiliar with Farmville. Farmville is a farming simulation game played primarily via Facebook, and more recently on iPhones and iPads. Launched by gaming company Zynga in 2009, Farmville quickly became the fastest-growing and most popular social game ever. During its first twenty-six weeks alone, Farmville added one million net new users per week, eventually reaching a hundred million users per month at its peak, before copycat games dented its popularity.[10]

These are the facts. If you don't play Farmville, you need to do some work to get to the idea-links. You could start playing the game yourself and pay attention to why it's addictive. Or you could ask other people who play Farmville why they play it. Or you can do what I did and simply Google "success of Farmville." If you do, numerous postings will pop up from pundits who were curious and motivated enough to share their "idea-links."

One of these postings, "The Six Secrets of Farmville's Success," theorizes that Farmville went viral partly due to "the joy and shame of gifting."[11] Open Farmville, and the first screen you'll encounter isn't your farm, but rather a list of gifts to give your friends, such as a sheep or a honeybee. In Farmville culture, these gifts actually carry value to the recipient. By encouraging gift giving and placing perceived value on the gifts, Farmville taps into something extremely powerful: The reciprocating nature of gift giving. In nearly every culture, when one person gives a gift, the other feels an obligation to reciprocate. By encouraging gift giving and allowing for easy reciprocity, Farmville taps into a human response thousands of years in the making. The result: A level of engagement and viral behavior far greater than other games.

If you know that Farmville grew to a hundred million users, you know a fact. If, however, you understand that part of the reason Farmville grew to a hundred million users is because they tapped into the reciprocating nature of gift-giving, you own an idea-link.

Finding idea-links at work

Let's take one final example, this time moving from your home life to your job. Since we all have different jobs, I'll set up a hypothetical situation. Let's say you're in charge of marketing baking products like flour or shortening. Over the years, as consumers have gotten busier and busier, they bake from scratch less often, and thus use fewer of your products. You're in the hot seat. How would you turn around the baking supply business? Where will the breakthrough ideas come from?

Now, let's pretend your friend or your mom is into scrapbooking, a relatively new pastime compared to baking, that's grown into a multi-billion-dollar business over the last ten years. You could stop at the facts: Scrapbooking is a growing industry that's now larger than the baking industry. Or you could seek to understand why and dig into what really drives interest in scrapbooking. As part of your digging, you might discover a few things: People love to scrapbook because they can make a unique and personal gift. People love to scrapbook because it allows them to leave a tangible legacy. People love to scrapbook because it's a fun, low-stress way to meet and socialize with other people.

These are all idea-links. They're realizations or insights about Why Scrapbooking is Popular that can be stored into your memory and connected to another problem. When you return to your problem, How to Grow the Baking Business, these idea-links hold the potential to lead you to new ideas, to new linkages.

Now look at the scrapbooking idea-links again, thinking about your baking objective. Are you already seeing ways to re-energize baking as a pastime? In fact, when you read "make a unique and personal gift" did you also think back to the Farmville idea-link and recall how the gift-giving aspect of the game took Farmville viral? When considering these idea-links, then relating them to the baking business, a promising idea emerges: What if we develop an integrated campaign encouraging (and helping) consumers to bake items they can give as gifts? And what if this give-baked-goods-as-gifts campaign triggers a reciprocating response?

When I first posed the challenge of reinvigorating the baking industry, the gift-giving idea wasn't there. When we thought about what caused other pastimes to grow, such as Farmville and scrapbooking, it was. The idea didn't come from out of the blue. It came from idea-links we stored away, just like it did for Steve Jobs.

You may be asking yourself how an idea-link differs from other kinds of memories you store away. Idea-links are specific kinds of memories that hold creative potential. They aren't facts, they're insights, realizations, or understandings about how or why something works or succeeds. Once a memory is stored as an insight or realization, it becomes transportable and highly connectable. In other words, it's free to link up with seemingly unrelated problems or disparate situations to create ideas. Facts can't do this, only idea-links.

"Scrapbooking or Farmville is growing" is a memory of a factual kind, but because the reason behind its growth has yet to be extracted (or mined), the fact itself holds no creative potential. The fact isn't "shaped" properly to connect to a new problem. It's only a fact. It's only through work and effort that it becomes an idea-link. Yes, idea-links must be manufactured. You *make* idea-links, and here's how.

The surprising role of analysis

This chapter began with the premise that creative people are doing something under the surface that makes them more creative than the rest of us; something so natural and unintentional they don't even realize they're doing it. I've introduced you to the concept of idea-links—the building blocks of creativity—and made the case that people who are good at generating ideas excel not because they were born with an extra idea chromosome, but because they've stored away lots of idea-links to work with. We all make idea-links; highly creative people simply make more of them. So what's the underlying skill behind the manufacture of idea-links? And what drives naturally creative people to make them in the first place?

Most people simply observe the world around them. Creative people analyze. Let me repeat that: Creative people analyze. It may be shocking to see "creative" and "analyze" in the same sentence, but it's the most important and eye-opening concept in this book. It was my breakthrough moment in understanding what makes me, and others, creative. Creative people analyze, and it's what and how they analyze that sets them apart.

Most people simply observe the world around them. Creative people analyze.

I have always sought to understand at a deeper level why things work or don't work. The idea-people I work with tell me the same thing, but most of us consider it unremarkable. Why? Because just as naturally organized people apply their organization principles instinctually, creative people naturally apply their creative principles to analyze why or how things work, or why people do what they do.

What drives this analytical energy? By now, you've probably guessed it: Curiosity. That's the innate talent, or gift, naturally creative people have in abundance. They go beyond what they see or hear (the facts) and seek to understand the *why*. It's the seeking of the *why* or the *how* that turns an everyday observation into a connectable thought, or idea-link.

Prior to reading this book, we could all probably agree on two things: Creative people are curious, and ideas come from making connections. What wasn't known? These two facts are linked by a hidden idea-link-manufacturing process. Curiosity drives analysis. Analysis creates idea-links. Idea-links serve as raw material for making connections.

How the "raw material" of creativity is manufactured

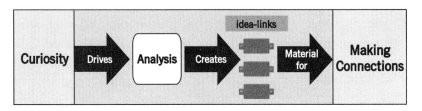

This revolutionary idea makes creativity accessible to everyone. Idea-links aren't just for a select few; they're available to all of us, all the time, every day, everywhere, lurking just under the surface. And because the process of unearthing these idea-links is an analytical exercise, anyone willing to undertake a little work can become more creative. You don't even need to be especially curious; you only need the awareness and motivation to dig a little deeper than you have in the past.

You might not care why people play Farmville or why scrapbooking became a multi-billion-dollar business seemingly overnight. I care because I'm naturally curious. I can't help but ask. But whether I do it innately or intentionally, my reward is the same: More idea-links in my bank for future use. If you're motivated to become more creative, you must ask questions, dig for answers, and analyze findings to manufacture your own raw material. To become more creative, the idea-link-manufacturing process is the first of two disciplines you must follow.

For those of you who think (or have been told) you're too analytical to be creative, or that somehow these two talents are contradictory, you now know the surprising truth: Creativity can't be built without analysis.

If, right now, you're shaking your head at that thought instead of nodding in agreement, you're probably still thinking about analysis the wrong way. Analyzing for creativity isn't like analyzing a financial statement to figure out your net worth. That kind of computational analysis seeks answers for immediate use. Analysis for the sake of creativity is different; you do it for the idea-link that may someday forge a new connection. That eventual connection may happen next week, sometime in the distant future, or never. On rare occasions, the analysis coincides closely with the aha moment, as was the case in my Farmville and baking-products example. But in most cases, the analysis occurs years before the idea is born. This delayed utility is the primary difference between analysis as you normally think of it, and analysis to make an idea-link.

Knowing this new relationship between analysis and creativity also means you and others can no longer claim you're too analytical to become creative. In fact, the opposite is true—you have the skills, you just need to apply your natural gift for analysis in a new and exciting way. Think back to Jack Gust, Paul Simon, and Lady Gaga. What were they doing to prepare for their aha moments? Having fun and acting playful? No, just the opposite. These creative geniuses were behaving in an analytical fashion. They analyzed their environment and areas relevant to their professions and deliberately extracted and stored idea-links for later use. You can do the same.

Making Idea-Links Is No Accident— It's a Choice

This new understanding of creativity also offers a better understanding of creative people. Highly creative people (for the most part) aren't undisciplined nut jobs who spout ideas randomly out of aloofness or lack of focus. Creative people are analytical powerhouses constantly scanning their environments to turn everyday observations into valuable creative assets. The creative assets now stored away in their brains—their idea-links—were manufactured through work. That highly creative people actually *enjoy* the process doesn't diminish the incredible value of the assets they produce.

Understanding *why* or *how* doesn't happen by itself. You have to choose to do the extra work, just like I had to choose to create places for my things to become more organized. The next step in your journey to greater creativity is to commit to doing more than you are now—choose to think harder and dig deeper.

Like any other skill, it won't come naturally at first, but I promise it will be worth the effort. Whether you're looking to broaden your creative horizons in a general sense, or you've got specific issues and need some fresh ideas ASAP, I can show you how to start building and cultivating your own bank of idea-links right now. Let's get going!

SIDETRACK: Not All Associations Are Created Equal

Every connection comes from associating one thing with another. But are some associations better than others?

Let's pretend it's 2002 and you're in charge of growing the coronary stent business (coronary stents are metal, tubelike structures inserted into coronary arteries to maintain blood flow). As part of an effort to find new product ideas, you go to a new product ideation session and the moderator tells you to open the dictionary and randomly point to a word. From that word, you're asked to come up with an idea for the stent business based on your associations with that word. If you pointed to "stop," you might think of a stop sign, which makes you think of "red," which leads to the idea for a red-colored stent. If you pointed at the word "seed," you might think of "corn" which could lead you to an idea for stents made from plant matter. Both ideas have little value, but they're added to a list on the wall nonetheless.

I refer to these kinds of associations—stop/red and seed/corn—as surface associations. Surface associations are the thoughts that come when you free-associate on a subject. I say "hamburger" and you free-associate "pickle," "mustard," "golden arches," etc. Many creative exercises encourage you to take these surface associations and try to connect them to your challenge.

Here's the problem with relying on surface associations for your creativity: They rarely lead to good ideas. You'll have to plow through lots of them before one triggers a workable idea. When workable ideas come from surface associations, they truly are ideas of serendipity. Relying on random surface associations to produce success is a highly impractical strategy; we need better control over our creativity than blindly pointing at random words and hoping for a magical connection.

Idea-links are a different kind of association that's much more valuable, controllable, and transportable. Think of an idea-link as a deep association. While surface associations come automatically and without work, deep associations come from analysis. They come from digging deeper. For example, if you had happened to analyze the seed industry, rather than just relying on your surface associations with the word itself, you might have remembered a key advance in seed technology. Some forty years ago, seeds were first coated with chemicals that made them more resistant to the hostile environment around them. The idea-link saved in your brain might sound something like this: **To help something survive in a hostile environment, pre-apply a resistant coating (coated seeds).**

If you went to the same coronary stent ideation and the moderator asked you instead, "What's your product category similar to?" you might then come up with the seed category, because both seeds and stents are inserted into an environment that's at once nurturing and hostile. You would focus on the word "seed" but only because it made sense. At that point, your idea-link about coated seeds pops into your head, helping you to create the nearly $6 billion coated stent business—a subcategory that didn't exist before 2003.

Since idea-links are shaped by the grit of analysis, they are considerably more connectable and valuable than surface associations.

The Old Creativity	The New Creativity
Analytical people can't be creative.	Analysis is critical to becoming more creative.
You must have fun to be creative.	Building your creativity will require some work and discipline.

3

Digging Deeper—Using Analysis to Create Idea-Links

American Idol debuted in the United States in 2002, and quickly became the most popular show in America, for at least a decade. Though its runaway popularity waned for a few years, a reinvigorated *American Idol* ended its tenth season with a bang, drawing 29.3 million viewers for its two-hour-plus finale.[12] Add in the original UK version, *Pop Idol*, plus *Britain's Got Talent,* plus the forty-three other spin-offs, and each year nearly a billion people will watch an *Idol*-format show, as they're now called. No show has ever taken the world by storm like *Idol*.[13]

Those are the facts. If you want to remain as creative as you are now, you stop at the facts and perhaps gain a few trivial statistics to toss around at a dinner party. However, if you want to become more creative, you have to dig a little bit deeper. What is it that makes *American Idol* so popular?

What's the secret behind the *Idol* phenomenon and can it be applied to categories other than television shows?

To make idea-links, you have to move beyond the fact that *American Idol* is (or was) a top TV show. If you aren't already naturally curious about the *why*, you need the discipline to analyze *why* anyway. Let me take this a step further: If you work in marketing, advertising, promotions, sales, or PR, it's your job to analyze why *American Idol* works. To leave one of the most popular shows on the planet unanalyzed for its idea-link potential is a crime against creativity. To save your job, we'll do this one together.

The Idol Formula

Extracting *Idol* idea-links takes some digging—not the jump-with-both-feet-on-the-shovel kind of digging, just a light raking to see what's happening underneath this phenomenon.

With a little pondering, the reasons behind the show's appeal reveal themselves. A hero rises from obscurity. A weekly contest creates winners and losers. The audience participates in selection to create a sense of allegiance to and investment in particular contestants. Mentors appear, in the form of celebrities such as Stevie Wonder and Gwen Stefani, to counsel and teach contestants. In its original version, the show leveraged a tension between Simon Cowell, the contestants' cranky nemesis, and his opposite, their loyal friend, Paula Abdul. In fact, you could say tension existed between Simon and practically everyone else—the judges, the host, the contestants, and the audience, both in-studio and watching at home.

If you're developing a television show, these are successful elements you can extract and apply to another show. Other networks discovered this and quickly jumped on the bandwagon with an assortment of *Idol* variants by applying combinations of these elements to everything from dance to modeling to cake-making.

But if you grab a Garden Weasel and dig a bit deeper, you'll unearth an even bigger idea-link. Yes, each individual element is part of *Idol's* success, but it's the way they all work together that's the biggest prize. Without Simon as the evil villain, you simply have another *Star Search*, the long-running show hosted by the late Ed McMahon, which never approached the popularity of *Idol*. There is something about how all the pieces work together that made *Idol* must-watch television.

Yes, the big idea-link is the *formula*, and for those of you who are literature majors or movie critics, you might recognize it as a classic literary framework, or as the story-telling structure mythologist Joseph Campbell dubbed "The Hero's Journey."[14,15] Here's what it looks like:

The Idol Formula

	American Idol
Hero	American Idol winner
Nemesis	Simon Cowell
Born in Obscurity	Unknown
Symbol of Power	Microphone
Mentor	Stevie Wonder, Bon Jovi, Diana Ross, et al
Friends	Other contestants; Paula
Test	America's votes

Congratulations! You've just created an idea-link to file away. You can call it classic heroic structure, the hero's journey, or you can just call it the *Idol* formula. What's most important? It works. When will you use it? You'll have creative access to this tried-and-true formula anytime you need a framework for making a product, person, brand, or story more appealing, engaging, or memorable. Where will you use it? That's up to you.

Taking Your Idea-Link Outside Your Category

Once you store away idea-links like Introduce a Nemesis or Apply the *Idol* Formula, they're ready for transport outside of television. Say you're developing a new promotion or publicity event for your product. What would happen if you considered *Idol*-based idea-links? What if you introduced a nemesis? Or a mentor? Or created a contest in which people vote—not just once, but over and over? Each individual element might lead you to a great idea.

Or you could reapply the entire formula. Want to write a best-selling book? This one might look familiar.

The Idol Formula

	Harry Potter
Hero	Harry Potter
Nemesis	Voldemort
Born in Obscurity	Lived with his aunt and uncle, parents murdered
Symbol of Power	Scar
Mentor	Dumbledore
Friends	Ron, Hermione
Test	Many

Need to create an engaging press release? Or tell an interesting brand story? None is better than the brand story of legendary sports beverage Gatorade. The memorable Keith Jackson–narrated "History of Gatorade" spot goes like this (notice the inclusion of the born-of-humble-origins element):

Jackson. The legend was born in 1965 in the storied Swamp of Florida, where the scorching heat took a brutal toll on the Gators.

Inventor. The players weren't adequately hydrated and their performance suffered.

Jackson. The answer: a new carbohydrate-electrolyte beverage created by University doctors.

Inventor. Naturally, we called our stuff Gator Aid.

Jackson. When they won the '67 Orange Bowl, Gatorade had arrived. Born of humble origins, proven to this day. The legend continues . . .[16]

The Idol Formula

	Gatorade
Hero	Gatorade
Nemesis	Heat/Dehydration
Born in Obscurity	"Born of humble origins"
Symbol of Power	Championship Trophy
Mentor/Creator	Inventors
Friends/Partners	Florida Gators
Test	Gators defeat heavily-favored LSU in 100-degree heat

Taking Simon to the Bake-Off

So now you see how a tried-and-true format, once it's filed away as an idea-link, can work for you again and again. Let's use it one more time—this time to improve a long-running, successful promotion like the Pillsbury Bake-Off.

The Bake-Off is already *Idol*-like in many ways, especially the "winner from obscurity" angle. But what could Pillsbury "steal" from *Idol* to make its success more like *Idol* and less like *Star Search*? One idea: Introduce a nemesis. I'm not suggesting you let Simon rip on some poor lady's cake. As entertaining as it might be to hear, "Sandra, your lemon cake is a complete and utter mess," Pillsbury has a reputation to uphold.

But what about time as nemesis? Or limited on-hand ingredients? These are the Simon Cowells that real-life cooks face every day. Make the contest more interesting by setting a time limit. Or an ingredient limit. Who can make the best dinner in less than ten minutes, or by using only five ingredients? It not only makes the contest more interesting, but also more relevant.

Once again, Hollywood—the master of recycling idea-links—jumped on it first. Nemesis as person: *Hell's Kitchen*. Nemesis as time: *Cake Boss*. Both are popular shows, but remove the nemesis and you have just another cooking show. They brought elements of the *Idol* formula to the cooking show format to create new ideas. And it worked.

Once you find an idea-link like the *Idol* formula, you can apply it anywhere—singers, dancers, brand stories, press releases, novels, baked goods, restaurants—even wedding dresses! One of my twelve-year-old daughter's favorite shows is *Say Yes to the Dress*. Listening to it in the background, my first reaction was dismay that they'd actually make an entire series about shopping for wedding dresses. When my daughter, Jayme, started recording episodes on our DVR, I figured that rather than dismiss it, I should put on my analytic hard hat and try to figure out what makes the show tick.

If you analyze the show's popularity, you'll see the *Idol* formula peeking out from behind the ruffles and lace. The contestants in this show aren't people, but dresses, each vying for the chance to appear in the most important day in each woman's life. But a show about someone trying on dresses is snooze city, even to my daughter. After all, they're just dresses. We don't even know who made the dresses and no one wins anything if their dress is the one selected. Now, think about the *Idol* formula. Is an idea coming to you about how to spice things up?

In each episode, the bride-to-be brings her entourage. And guess which characters appear in her entourage? There's the amiable friend who's supportive no matter how hideous a dress looks, but who frustrates you to no end because she provides no usable knowledge or guidance (think Paula Abdul). And then there's her evil counterpart, the snotty, opinionated villain who rips on the dresses, humiliates the bride, and demeans other members of the bride's posse, but who provides some sense of relief to the viewer because she actually helps the bride move closer to her selection. Sound like someone you know?

File the *Idol* idea-link away. But first, think about how you can apply the idea-link of villain or nemesis to sell your product, service, or company in a way that's more appealing, more engaging, or even more heroic. And next time you watch your favorite television show, don't just watch it;

think about *why* you watch it. You'll find idea-links buried in every successful show. In fact, *American Pickers, Storage Wars, Pawn Stars,* and *Antique Roadshow* all share the same idea-link. If you take a moment right now to make it, you'll be more creative than you were before you read this sentence.

Prius Envy

Let's turn our attention to another runaway success from the last decade: The Toyota Prius. What juicy idea-links does the Prius offer?

Start by finding out what people love about these cars. Go to Google and type in "why I love my Prius" or better yet, ask the guy down the street who glides silently past your home every morning. When it comes to the Prius, you can even ask a complete stranger. Prius owners aren't shy about sharing the intimate details of their hybrid love affair. While conducting your research, avoid the temptation to stop at the obvious. "Because it gets good gas mileage" is a fact with no connective value. If that's the response you get, simply counter with, "Lots of cars get good gas mileage. What was it in particular about the Prius?" Again, only by digging deeper can you get to the good stuff.

So what is it about the Prius? First, let's talk design. Toyota introduced the Prius around the same time as Honda introduced their Civic Hybrid. Both get excellent gas mileage and both are built by well-respected manufacturers. So why did the Prius clobber the Civic Hybrid in sales, despite Civic's strong brand equity?

In short, Toyota designed the Prius to look *different* from other cars, while Honda designed the Civic Hybrid to look *the same* as its conventional counterpart. Toyota apparently wanted their hybrid to stand out, while Honda wanted theirs to blend in. At first blush, the Honda strategy seems smarter. The traditional Civic is a successful vehicle with a well-researched and widely desired design. Why wouldn't Honda leverage both the brand equity and the design equity, especially when new hybrid technology was already a risky venture?[17]

What Honda didn't consider adequately (or failed to predict) was human nature. Many hybrid buyers possess a need far stronger than the desire to save money. In a 2007 study, 57% of Prius owners said their main reason for buying was that "it makes a statement about me." Only 36% cited fuel economy as the primary motivator.[18] In other words, for many Prius owners, showing other people they care about the environment outweighs the desire to curb greenhouse gas emissions or save money. It's a need Honda didn't consider, or at least didn't take seriously enough. If you design a car that looks like a conventional car, you rob buyers of their opportunity to make a statement. But give them something that screams, "Look at me! I'm driving a car that proves I care about the environment," and they'll snap them up by the millions.

Here's the idea-link: **When developing green products (that are seen by other people), designing them to look different fulfills consumers' need to communicate their values to others.** A more succinct expression might be: **To help consumers make a social statement, give them a visible means of expression.**

When will you use this idea-link? Well, certainly while working on any kind of green initiative. But a link like this can extend beyond green. How might it apply to other products or services where consumers desire to outwardly express their values to others? Think about Tom's Shoes, a popular fashion item among the twenty-something set. For every pair of shoes Tom's sells, they give a pair to someone in need. In a four-year span, Tom's donated 600,000 shoes, meaning they've likely sold $33 million worth of cloth shoes over that same time period (at $55 a pop). But Tom's Shoes wouldn't have near this success were it not for the uniqueness of the shoes themselves. The distinctive look, shape, and material of Tom's Shoes say to the outside world, "Look, these are Tom's Shoes; they show I care about other people." Take away the uniqueness and you lose the outward expression.

I've had people say to me, "Yeah, but what if Toyota never intended for the Prius to look different? What if its unique shape resulted from the engineers' need to make it aerodynamic, not because the marketers wanted to help people make a statement?"

I don't know if it was intentional or not. But my response is the same either way: It doesn't matter. Regardless of Toyota's original intent, the fact remains that having a design that stands apart from conventional products helps people make a social statement, and it's a big part of the Prius success story. Whether Toyota did this on purpose or by accident is irrelevant. The idea-link holds the same value.

The Addictive Power of Immediate Feedback

Let's grab another Prius-based idea-link while we're at it. Normally, when you think about a car that's fun to drive, you think of features like handling, acceleration, a great sound system, or a convertible top. But since when is "getting great gas mileage" a fun factor? It is with the Prius. In fact, an entire social network now exists for owners to share the secrets of skimping.

The biggest of these social networks is the website PriusChat.com. Here's a posting I grabbed randomly:

> I made my first trip in my 2003 Prius and it was 250 miles each way from LA to Vegas. I got the standard Prius 46 mpg on the trip there. But the return trip it was another story. I made a coffee stop and topped off the tank in Barstow. It only took $6.30, which is a little over two gallons here. And then I drove all the way back to Los Angeles and it still shows a full tank. There was a downhill stretch that lasted forty minutes to an hour where I was using almost no gas at all. And it was then I started to discover by dropping the cruise control one mile an hour at a time I could keep the electric engine handling most of the work. I'd say if I topped it off now, I am guessing it would take 5 bucks. That means I got home on a little over eleven dollars in gas. Less than four gallons. That's 70-80 mpg! Plus I was driving 70 and had the A/C on for a lot of the trip.[19]

To us non-Prius owners, reading postings like this is like watching paint dry, but to Prius owners, it's penny-pinching porn. Spend a few minutes on PriusChat.com or any of the countless other websites or blogs, and you'll see thousands of stories just like this. The Prius spawned a worldwide community of misers who like nothing better than to find every trick in the book to squeeze a few more inches out of every drop of gas. It's a community Prius drivers refer to as "The Fellowship of the Prius."[20] Join it, and you'll learn terms like "Pulse and Glide" and "Burn and Coast." Get sucked in too far and you might join the ranks of the "hypermilers"—mileage fanatics who obsess over ways to reach 100 miles per gallon or more.

Why are Prius drivers, in particular, so nutty about sharing mileage? Other cars get decent gas mileage, so what's different here? The difference, simply, is feedback. When the Prius was introduced, it didn't just give you an odometer and a gas gauge, like other vehicles of the time. Prius created the first real-time, LED-lit shrine to mileage tracking. Want to know how much gas you just used and compare it to a previous trip? Prius will tell you. How about gas usage and mileage in the past five minutes? They'll give you that, and if you push another button, you'll get the same report, but this time for the last minute. Real-time graphs. Detailed analyses. All designed to appeal to our inner geek.

Even more ingenious, the dash tells you how much energy you recaptured through regenerative braking. Put another way: How much gas you just received for free. It's like winning a small-scale lottery every time you go down a hill. For Prius owners, this kind of positive feedback is highly addictive, but in a good way. It's the kind of feedback that encourages Prius drivers to find new ways to get even better mileage, and then share their finds with others.

So here's the idea-link: **Providing real-time, understandable feedback motivates people to save because it becomes addictive.**

Another way of saying it might be: **Real-time feedback on cost-savings is fun, addictive and motivating.**

You might put it differently, and that's okay. But this wording works for me and as you'll see shortly, it's transportable. An idea-link, worded this way, can now be applied or connected to a different problem and create an even bigger idea. It's just there, waiting for the right problem to come along.

Reapplying Your Prius Idea-Link

Let's pretend now that the Department of Energy (DOE) has chosen you, the most creative person in your town or city, to help find a way to decrease energy usage. One area the DOE is interested in exploring is home energy usage. They want to know how they can encourage people to save gas and electricity in their homes. And they're looking to you for a creative solution. Now slow down for a bit and focus on the problem: Finding creative ways to motivate people to save gas and electricity in their homes.

Is the idea coming to you yet? Do you see how when you hear the words "motivate" or "save," the second Prius idea-link barges right in and sparks an idea that seems obvious in hindsight? If providing real-time, understandable feedback encourages consumers to use less gas in their cars, shouldn't the same feedback work in their homes? Come to think of it, isn't it ridiculous that there's no way to read our meters ourselves? Even if we had the gumption to read our own meters, what would we see? A bunch of dials spinning around? When it comes to energy feedback, the Prius gives us easy-to-read, up-to-the-second data. But the controls that utility and electric companies provide for our homes are the industry equivalent of medieval sundials.

What would happen if you had a feedback center in your home to tell you in real-time that turning off the kitchen lights drops your energy cost from eighteen to sixteen cents per minute? Do you think you'd turn those lights off more often? Or, what if, when you switch on your outdated gas fireplace, your feedback center tells you that the lost heating efficiency (versus your furnace) costs an additional seven dollars an hour? Would you still think that pretty fire was worth it? Maybe, if you've just poured a glass of wine to share with your significant other who just returned from a business trip. Maybe not, if you're just going to sit in another room and update your Facebook page.

What if that twenty-minute shower your teenage son took to "wake up" spits out a receipt for twenty dollars? Tack that receipt on his door, ask for ten dollars back and I guarantee those long showers will be a thing of the past.

What can people do with all this information? What could happen if the Prius effect literally hits home? People might begin to tinker with the various factors that could save energy; they might even find the tinkering addictive. Before long, they'd probably go online to share their tips with others. Not everyone, but some. Just like the Prius owners.

By the way, here's one more idea for the Department of Energy. When you make these in-home monitors, make them look noticeably different from current thermostats and put them in prominent locations. When homeowners have their friends over, they'll want to make a social statement.

Preparing Your Mind with Idea-Links

Do you see now the power of idea-links taken from your everyday experiences? You may have heard the famous Louis Pasteur quote, "Chance favors the prepared mind." Filing away these Prius idea-links "prepares" your mind for the moment when the right problem presents itself. We just had one of those exhilarating aha moments together, but only because we had the raw material at the ready from our Prius analysis. Were we being playful and wacky? Were we "unleashing" something innate but long suppressed? No. We just did a little bit of analytical work to prepare our minds to be more creative. We set up our aha moment by making idea-links.

The great thing about idea-links is that the best ones, like the ones we just made, are often recyclable. Preparing your mind

Preparing your mind with idea-links pays regular creative dividends.

with idea-links pays regular creative dividends. Here's an example. I'll give you a new objective; this time I need you to create a new kind of traffic sign to motivate people to slow down in a residential neighborhood. Hearing the word "motivate" links me back to the Prius idea-link: **real-time, understandable feedback is a motivator to get people to change their behavior.** How does this idea-link prepare your mind for a new problem outside of the realm of energy savings? Take a moment to consider what type of immediate, under-standable feedback might motivate you to slow down.

On my way to work each morning is a traffic sign where the speed limit abruptly drops from fifty-five to thirty m.p.h. as I enter a residential area. Above the sign announcing the drop to thirty is a flashing readout telling me how fast I'm going (or when I jog past it, sadly, how slow I'm going). It's a decent reminder, but I'll be the first to admit, I take chances here and there, even with the feedback.

What if we created a sign that provided data that was a bit more compelling? What unit of measurement would provide a better motivation to change my behavior than knowing my actual driving speed? Got an idea yet? Here's mine: What if a sign took your speed, calculated the amount over the speed limit, then displayed the amount of your fine, rather than the extent of your speed? Would you be more likely to slow down if the sign was flashing $147? I would!

The speed is the same. We've simply taken a Prius idea-link and reapplied it in a way that made the sign's feedback have a greater impact on your behavior. That's really all Toyota did with the Prius: Change the feedback to have a greater impact on behavior. We simply analyzed, extracted, and reapplied what Toyota already did. But before we could analyze, we first had to notice the Prius as a potentially rich source of idea-link deposits.

From Attention Deficit to Attention Requisite

As inventors go, Sir Isaac Newton did pretty well. He invented or explained little things like gravity, the laws of motion, differential and integral calculus, momentum, reflecting telescopes, and the visible spectrum of light. Was Newton a seventeenth-century smarty-pants and idea-link-making guy, too? Let's look to his own words for an answer: "If I have ever made any valuable discoveries, it has been owing more to patient attention than to any other talent." So there you go. Sounds like idea-link thinking, Enlightenment-style.

Patient attention and analysis is what making idea-links is all about. Extracting the idea-links from *American Idol* required us to first notice its idea-link-possessing potential, then analyze what makes it tick. Same thing goes for the Prius. Same goes for Jobs's study of calligraphy. Once you realize that idea-link creation starts with paying careful attention, you'll begin to see that it's part of the secret behind what we call "creative genius."

Comedian Steve Martin didn't invent gravity, but if he had, he would've found a way to make it funny, or at least interesting. In 2005, Martin received the Mark Twain Prize for American Humor. If you're not familiar with his humor, watch his acceptance speech on YouTube.[21] In Martin's autobiography, *Born Standing Up,* he unveils the secret that transformed his career from struggling magician to rising comedian.

> I kept scrupulous records of how each gag played after my local shows for the Cub Scouts or Kiwanis Club. "Excellent!" or "Big laugh!" or "Quiet," I would write in the margins of my Big Indian tablet; then I would summarize how I could make the show better next time. I was still motivated to do a magic show with the standard patter, but the nice response to a few gags had planted a nagging thought that contradicted my magical goal: They love it when the tricks don't work.[22]

This realization emerged from Martin's careful analysis of what worked and what didn't. The idea-link he extracted— people laugh when the tricks don't work—formed the foundation for Martin's early comedy. Martin continued to work hard at the comedy business, paying careful attention to the comedic elements that garnered the biggest laughs, and using them to refine his craft.

Creative success didn't come easily for Martin; making it big wasn't about being playful or letting himself feel free. He wasn't born a creative genius. He didn't wait for aha moments. Martin's creative success stemmed from the same type of "patient attention" and deep analysis as Newton's.

The same is true for director Quentin Tarantino, considered to be among our generation's most innovative filmmakers. Tarantino, a high-school dropout with no film school experience, gathered his creative raw material while working in a video store in California, intently studying and systematically analyzing everything from Italian B movies to classic films.[23] As he puts it, "When people ask if I went to film school, I tell them 'no, I went to films.'"[24] If you're a movie buff, you'll see the elements he extracted from his extensive film study surface again and again. (Watch *Everything is a Remix: Kill Bill* on YouTube for a vivid demonstration).

So what kind of patient attention should you develop? That depends on your job. Some years back, I conducted a new product ideation for the industrial respirator team at 3M. As we were planning the session, the discussion moved toward the invitees. I wondered aloud if they'd be creative. "Don't worry," I was told, "the most creative guy in the division is coming." Intrigued by this creative legend, I couldn't wait to see what ideas he would produce.

He didn't disappoint. Turns out this guy knew everything about breathing. Not just humans, but fish, horses, amoebas, plants, you name it. If it took in one kind of gas and expelled another, this guy knew how it happened. The rest of us in the room knew that fish had gills, but this guy understood precisely how gills worked. He also noticed how racehorses could extract additional oxygen by flaring their nostrils, which made a lot of sense in hindsight, but had never occurred to the rest of us.

Worthless trivia or valuable idea-links? Understanding how gills work, and their orientation on a fish in relation to the fish's mouth, led to the idea of moving the filters back on the respirator, farther away from direct contact with contaminants (such as paint) that shorten filter life. Flaring horse nostrils led to the idea of a power boost of air, which the wearer could summon on command under strenuous breathing conditions.

How would you describe the secret of the most creative guy in the room? Was he born more creative? Did he pop out of the birth canal explaining how gills work and how racehorse nostrils flare? What separates the highly creative from their counterparts isn't all that mysterious.

Why a Little Stealing Is a Good Thing and a Lot of Stealing Is a Great Thing

Picasso once said, "Good artists borrow; great artists steal." Let me say right off that I'm not advocating stealing ideas. I've had lots of mine stolen and I'm sure I've inadvertently stolen those of others. Sometimes we hear an idea and forget where we heard it, or we make a subtle change and think of it as our own. Mistakes happen.

But make no mistake; I'm a huge fan of stealing *idea-links*. When great artists like Picasso, Paul Simon, and Quentin Tarantino steal from others, they aren't stealing the painting, the song, or the movie. That's plagiarism. Instead, they're extracting what works and reapplying it in their own unique way, in their own field. That's creativity. In fact, so much has Paul Simon "stolen" from other sources that he modestly confesses in a *Rolling Stone* article, "I never invented anything."[25] If our greatest living songwriter feels he never invented anything, perhaps none of us have.

We all rearrange what's in our heads. The trick is getting more of the right stuff in there. So, for example, if you're looking to become a more creative designer, start "stealing" appealing design principles everywhere you go. From billboards. From cereal boxes. From nature. From paintings. From baseball stadiums. From websites. If you do, you might notice what I did when I analyzed why Apple's websites and packages feel different: They don't use black and white; they use off-black on a soft, matte white background. That subtle difference in shading is a design idea-link I've stolen from the world of web and package design and reapplied to book design. When I combined my design idea-links with the design idea-links contributed by my design team, we created a new design. We were creative. And I was more creative at design than most authors (or so they told me) because I had taken the time to notice the world of design and mentally extract what works.

I also did a good bit of research on the process of writing books. One of these reference books, *From Book Idea to Bestseller* by Michael Snell, spelled out what quality separated good writers from the rest. "Good writers," Snell begins, "read other writers, but unlike people who read for the sheer pleasure of it, *they read analytically*, trying to figure out exactly how the author achieved that absorbing effect on the page. Good architects don't just admire a beautiful house; they analyze the elements that contributed to its style."[26]

Without knowing it, Snell is also describing what sets the creative apart from the not-so-creative. "Analyzing the elements" is the same as creating, extracting, and, yes, stealing idea-links. The more elements of "absorbing effect" a writer has accumulated in her head, the more creative she'll become in crafting her next book.

Same with the architect.

Same with the designer.

And the marketers who took a break from pie charts and bar graphs and instead analyzed *American Idol* for its winning elements will generate more creative marketing ideas than the ones who watched it for entertainment alone. They're no smarter or mentally adept than the average *Idol* viewer, they merely worked a little bit harder and dug a tad deeper. And they were rewarded with idea-links that enhanced their creative potential. Picasso was right. Great artists do steal.

The Old Creativity	The New Creativity
Be wacky and playful.	Pay attention and analyze.

4

Curiosity—Getting Your "Why" Back

I have no special talent.
I am only passionately curious.

—ALBERT EINSTEIN, SCIENTIST

If you're reading this book on a tablet, laptop computer, or e-reader, you can thank a guy by the name of Andy Ouderkirk for your device's bright screen and long battery life. More accurately, you can thank his curiosity.

Because he's a corporate scientist with 3M's Film/ Light Management Technology Center, Ouderkirk casts his curiosity into the world of light and color around him and catches little things the rest of us miss. Most of us simply go for a walk; Ouderkirk goes for a walk and notices the unique way light passes through the wings of a butterfly and wonders why. Most of us pick up rocks and toss them; Ouderkirk picks up a rock and wonders how a fire opal gets its fire.

For highly creative people like Ouderkirk, natural curiosity powers the kind of analysis that leads to new realizations (idea-links) that can be reapplied or connected elsewhere. Ouderkirk discovered that a butterfly's wing gets its color not from pigment, but from light reacting with highly intricate patterns layered on the wing. This interaction between light and pattern produces brilliant hues that change with the angle of light. As Ouderkirk later discovered, the same holds true with the colors found in peacocks, blue jays, and rainbow trout. Even fire opals.

When Ouderkirk sought to reapply his idea-link to the challenge of making televisions, computers, and handheld devices brighter, he was greeted with skepticism. "Nothing that small and intricate could ever be manufactured artificially," he was told. Responding with the kind of innovative spirit for which 3M is famous, Ouderkirk proclaimed, "If a butterfly can figure it out, so can we." And so they did.

By stacking extraordinarily thin layers of film, 3M found a way to mimic the same intricate structure found in a butterfly's wing. How many layers? The optical film on your laptop is as thin as a piece of paper, yet is made of nearly 900 layers of film. If you're reading this paragraph on one of those old-fashioned books made of paper, stop reading and look at this page from its side, and then try to imagine 900 layers fitting within that width. The film created by Ouderkirk and his coworkers at 3M reflects up to 99.5 percent of light, allowing light to be transported at efficiencies never before possible. So while you may not see all the layers, what you do see is an incredibly clear and vivid image that uses very little electricity.

Ouderkirk's curiosity and his team's perseverance put a profitable twist on the famous "butterfly effect"; when a butterfly flapped its wings in St. Paul, it made a computer screen brighter in China.

• • •

In 2008, I gave a speech on The New Creativity at a conference of communications and public relations professionals in Seattle. The opening keynote speaker was a top communications executive from Starbucks who shared stories of her company's recent PR successes. One story was so memorable that you may know it, especially if you're one of the millions of people whose daily routine requires Starbucks coffee.

In January 2008, the company's founder and former CEO, Howard Schultz, returned to Starbucks after an eight-year hiatus, appalled at an apparent slip in product quality during his absence. His first order of business: Retrain the baristas to make a cup of coffee to Schultz's exacting standards. But Schultz's objective wasn't just to do the training. He wanted to make a bold statement to his company, his customers, and the world that Starbucks was all about quality coffee. Rather than issuing a press release saying Starbucks would conduct retraining over the next few months, Schultz went for impact. He ordered all Starbucks closed for the same three-hour period on February 23, 2008, for "retraining." The press jumped on the story and by the end of the day, anyone who had stopped by a shuttered Starbucks, or opened their newspaper, or watched the news, knew that Starbucks customers could count on them for quality coffee.

When it was my turn to speak later that day, I asked the audience of two hundred PR professionals how many of them made note of the Starbucks retraining. Nearly all raised their hands. I then asked how many had written in their notes (or even thought about) *why* the retraining worked so well as a way to generate massive free publicity. This was, after all, an audience full of PR professionals. This time, just a few raised their hands. Nearly all had missed all the wonderful idea-links that they might reapply to their own business after they left the conference.

What wonderful idea-links had the conference participants missed? What had made Schultz's idea work so well? One was the use of **mass coordination to create an impact**. To say "at some point over the next three months your local Starbucks may close for retraining" isn't newsworthy. When you spread the training out over a period of time, the impact dissolves. Do it all at once, and you have news. Think flash mob with a mission.

But there's another idea-link here: **Demonstrating the willingness to hurt your own business is a great way to create news—and show you're serious.** Had Schultz sent his baristas to a training center, or conducted the training after hours, the story would have been a yawner. That's what you'd expect from a national chain. But closing all 11,000 stores during working hours is the kind of madness—and genius—that doesn't just make news but makes a huge impact. We can only wonder how much money was lost over those hours across all those stores—clearly they must be serious about quality!

So in an audience of two hundred bright, motivated individuals, all looking to become more creative at generating publicity, everyone took note of the fact—*what* Starbucks did. Only a few recorded the *why*, the reason it worked. Why did so few think past the *what* to the *why*? Were they too busy? Not likely. They were a captive audience—none of them were going anywhere. So why didn't they ask why?

Perhaps we need to raise the larger question: Why did we all stop asking why? We were all born curious to some extent or another, so what inhibits our innate curiosity? And maybe more importantly, can we get curiosity back or even build our curiosity to become the Andy Ouderkirks of our chosen fields?

I've posed this first question, Why Did We Stop Asking Why, to my audiences over the years and landed on two primary culprits. The first, curiosity isn't valued or emphasized by the organizations we work for, or worse, it's unwittingly devalued. The second, as organizations increase their focus on execution, there's no time or energy left for curiosity.

Where's Curiosity on Your Performance Review?

As kids, we asked *why* all the time, to various degrees. But something happened between the time we repeatedly posed that basic question as a child and the time we assumed our role as corporate ladder–climbers. As individuals working for a corporation, or any organization, we learn to behave intelligently based upon what that organization values.

If you want to know what your organization values, you need only open your performance appraisal. Or, if you think performance appraisals are a time-wasting sham (as most people do), it's better to take an honest look at the qualities possessed by the people who get promoted. If they're moving forward because they're great at execution, the people below them learn to become great executers. Or maybe it's decisiveness that your company values. If so, you can bet your decisive leaders will spawn decisive underlings.

But there's no grade for curiosity. In fact, it's not even a category on the report card. We get promoted for what we know, not for what we're curious about. Dig out your latest performance appraisal and see if there's a category that would laud the time Ouderkirk spent thinking about butterfly wings or rock hunting for opals in Idaho.

I recently got one of those "Can you talk to a friend-of-a-friend-of-a-friend who needs career advice?" calls. Here's a young woman, early twenties, in her first job in sales and marketing at a large corporation. She's graduated with a 3.9 GPA from a top-notch college, and she's a hard worker. Her intelligence and work ethic aren't in dispute on her performance appraisal, nor are her exceptional people skills. Her manager's complaint: She asks too many questions. "He tells me I ask too many questions, and I guess he's right, I do," she lamented. "I'm just so curious. I want to know why sales works the way it does; why we do certain things in the first place. But no one wants to hear those questions; they're like 'just get it done.' I'm starting to think I'm not cut out for a career in business."

A scene worthy of *The Office*? Yep. An unusual case? Unfortunately, no. Here's the paradox. All the managers and executives in a rush for their people to become more creative (and their teams to become more innovative) are failing to reward, and in some cases are punishing, the one quality that will most help their people be both more creative and innovative: curiosity. We need to see curiosity not as a weakness, or as evidence that someone isn't sure of the answer. We need to see curiosity as strength—evidence that some people have the courage to "put themselves out there" for the sake of creating or uncovering the idea-link that may eventually lead to an innovative idea.

If companies are serious about innovation, performance appraisal comments like "frequently takes time to question what makes things work and reapplies that learning to creatively solve business problems" and "frequently asks challenging and provocative questions" need to become as important as "can quickly and efficiently marshal resources to implement plans."

We get what we reward. Reward execution and we get people focused on execution. Reward the kind of curiosity-driven questioning and analysis that results in idea-links, and we get people who'll spend the time needed to become more creative.

Crowding Out Curiosity

Focus on execution is the other thief of our curiosity. When we become obsessively focused on execution—whether it's rolling out a new product, meeting challenging billing quotas at our law firm, or trying to handle a classroom of thirty-five kids—we miss things. The brain can only hold so much information in working memory, and if that memory is consumed by managing tasks and details, there's little bandwidth available for paying attention to the idea-links around us. Total focus on execution narrows our view of the world around us and limits our ability to build creativity.

This is best demonstrated in the book *Deep Survival*, a fascinating read by Laurence Gonzales, which seeks to explain how the brain works (or doesn't) under stressful survival conditions—the very conditions many of us feel in our jobs. It references one study where a group of Harvard psychologists put human attention to the test under somewhat bizarre conditions. Two groups of subjects watched a video of two teams passing a basketball. One team wore white, the other wore black. One group of subjects was instructed to count the number of passes between members of the white team. The other group wasn't given a task; the instructions were to just watch the video and report what they saw. At some point in the video, a person in a gorilla costume strolls through the center of the game and remains clearly visible for nearly five seconds, before exiting the court.

At the end of the study, a researcher asked subjects from the group that was asked to count passes, "Did you see anyone walking across the screen?" No, they hadn't. "Anything at all?" Nothing. When asked if they'd noticed the gorilla, the observers would say, "The *what*?" In fact, fifty-six percent of the pass-counting observers failed to notice the gorilla. Yet, the control group that wasn't asked to count passes easily spotted the gorilla. So what's the difference? And more importantly, what's the point?

According to Gonzales, the order "count the passes" produces a closed system, a narrowing of attention directed at a particular task, which fills up working memory. The demands of the task—largely one of execution—use up scarce brain resources. But "tell me what you see" produces curiosity. The second group watched the video with the attitude "What's up? What might I see there?" and easily found the gorilla in their midst.[27]

So here's the point: A total focus on execution crowds out curiosity, and if creativity is dependent on curiosity, well . . . you can see part of the reason we haven't become any more creative at work over the past twenty years. But to say "let's eliminate our focus on execution" is to live in denial. We have to get things done and we're all being asked to do more in less time. So how do we thrive in a world that demands both increased creativity and execution? Can these two somehow coexist?

Think of the problem as being something like texting and driving. If you try to do them at the same time, you can't do either very well (even if your teenager is convinced otherwise). But if you set aside time for texting when you're not in the car, you can fit both into your day. If returning a text is important to you, and you're prohibited from doing it while driving, you'll schedule a time in your day to get your texting done. Likewise, the only way to build your creativity is to set aside some "what do I see?" time amidst your "count the passes" day.

If you're leading a team, you can't just say, "we need to be more creative or more innovative," and expect it to happen. You need to have a plan. Then you need to set aside time to make it happen. If, say, you want your people to be more creative, you have to decide whether you mean it or you don't. To simply say, we need to be more creative, then expect it to happen is like telling a football team they need to be stronger without giving them time away from watching film to lift weights. The only way to fit in the idea-link-making "what do I see" behavior is to put it on equal footing with your other execution tasks. Think that's impossible? Meet Joe Ens.

Scheduling Time for Curiosity

Joe Ens is a vice president of marketing in the Food Service Division of General Mills. Ens's team of nearly fifty employees manages a dizzying array of brands and product sizes for a diverse group of customers ranging from elementary schools and corporate cafeterias to upscale restaurants and airlines. All of these groups depend on Ens's team to get them the right product in the right amount at the right time. In the food service business, execution is everything.

At the end of one of my workshops, Ens concluded, "If creativity is about making idea-links, and idea-links come from curiosity, this means I need to mandate curiosity." If mandating curiosity sounds counter to everything you ever thought about creativity, that's good. The book is subtitled *The New Creativity* for a reason. If creativity is about making idea-links, but a focus on execution crowds out the curiosity to make idea-links, then the only way to increase creativity is to forcibly carve out the time—or as Ens puts it, to *mandate* the time for the kind of behavior that will increase creativity.

While others may have attempted to carve out time to build creativity in the past, they lacked a clear idea of what to actually do during that time. Understanding the role of idea-links in creativity gives a clear direction for how to spend time, as a group, learning to generate and apply these links. You just need the will and leadership of a Joe Ens to make it happen.

Ens dubbed his effort Project Curiosity. There is now a large board in the office where people can post their findings. Each month, someone from the Project Curiosity Team suggests a new subject area for analysis. Being Minnesotans, a recent subject was State Fair Food—understanding what makes fair food so appealing, either the food itself or the environment in which it's eaten. Idea-links are gathered and later reviewed as a way to trigger new ideas. Each month, a new area, and each month, new idea-links. More importantly, the team now regularly practices the process of using their curiosity to mine idea-links from the world around them. With practice, making idea-links becomes second nature. The curiosity muscle grows stronger, the instinct more natural. Before long, team members begin finding idea-links outside of the regularly scheduled idea-link-making slot.

Ens forces his people out of their normal execution mode—counting the passes—and into extraction mode: What do I see here? By willfully moving yourself from execution to extraction mode, you gain a more mindful view of the world around you, coupled with a deep inquisitiveness to understand how and why things tick.

Can You Become More Curious on Your Own?

What if you don't have an enlightened boss like Joe Ens mandating and carving out curiosity time for you and your coworkers? Is there a way you can make yourself a more curious person? You can, but you may need to change some behaviors.

First, make a mental effort to reintroduce *why* into your regular thought process. This may seem both overly simplistic and impossible. It is, and it isn't. It's overly simplistic, because simple concepts stick. But it isn't impossible, or even difficult. For example, if you want to become a better conversationalist, and are motivated to improve, you could learn to say something like "tell me more" in the middle of conversations as a way of extending and enriching the conversation. You'd have to make a mental effort at first, but in a short time, it would become a matter of habit. Easy.

Likewise, you can learn to ask yourself or others "why" when you see or hear something interesting. It's not any more difficult than saying "tell me more," just different. "Tell me more" encourages conversation with others; "why" encourages curiosity within yourself. And curious behavior, as I've shown earlier, begins the process of becoming more creative. You may have lost some of your *why* over time, but you can get your *why* back if you try.

Judgment isn't only the opposite of curiosity, it's the mortal enemy of curiosity.

Finally, take a long, hard look at your tendency to judge. Judgment isn't only the opposite of curiosity, it's the mortal enemy of curiosity. Judgment of any kind short-circuits curiosity before it even has a chance to emerge. If, for example, I told you the facts of the Starbucks training story, and you responded with any of the following . . .

I don't watch the news.

I don't drink coffee.

I don't go to Starbucks.

Who cares?

Starbucks sucks.

I think people who pay four dollars for a cup of coffee are idiots.

. . . then you're probably a judger, or as I call them "judge-holes."

What's a judge-hole? I coined the term and added it to UrbanDictionary.com to define people who ruin an interesting story or idea with their own judgment, killing it in its tracks before anything valuable might get extracted. We're all judge-holes from time to time—situational judge-holes who unwittingly kill the creative process—but some make it part of their persona. Total judge-holes.

If you're a judger, and you know it, catch yourself and replace your judgment with something more curiosity-based such as, "I wonder why they did that," or "why did that make the news?" Curious questions of any kind open the door to analysis; judgment slams it shut. You can still sound just as cynical (you need to be yourself, after all) while saying something productive like, "That's stupid, I wonder why they did that." The last part of the phrase will at least move the conversation toward some type of analysis.

The only way to gather idea-links is to navigate life wearing your *why* hat, not your judge-hole hat. If you've lost your *why* over time, it's time to reclaim it, even though your organization may have unwittingly beat it out of you. If you've never been much of a *why* person, it's time to give it a try. You'll be amazed at all the little things you start noticing and the idea-links they produce.

And then you'll need a place to store them all.

SIDETRACK: The Curious Case of Asperger's Syndrome

There is some debate in autism circles about whether Asperger's syndrome (AS) is a type of autism, or simply on the higher-functioning end of an autism spectrum. But most agree that those living with Asperger's often possess above-average intelligence and generally function well in society. They just function differently. Some areas are more challenging, such as the ability to read social cues or express empathy, whereas in other areas, they possess natural advantages. One of those advantages is an ability to see problems differently and arrive at novel solutions.

In fact, some of history's most important contributors to mathematics, the sciences, and the arts have been posthumously diagnosed with AS based on recorded characteristics. Since such diagnoses are speculation, I'll leave it up to you to Google it and make your own determination. In the process, you'll also see many contemporary creative superstars who also match the AS criteria and are thus believed to be "on the spectrum" as well.

So what makes those with Asperger's syndrome creative? There is no definitive answer, but some recent work by noted autism researcher Professor Simon Baron-Cohen of the University of Cambridge suggests that those with AS find novel solutions because what they analyze differs from what their neuro-typical peers study.[28]

But here's the curious kicker: Those with AS actually score below average on standard creativity tests, such as the Torrance Test of Creative Thinking.[29] The Torrance test evaluates subjects' flexibility and originality and asks questions like, "How many different uses can you come up with for a tin can?" AS subjects score below average on these types of questions, particularly those that require imagination-based answers. So what is the test failing to measure?

Baron-Cohen found in a later study that those with AS excel at systemizing.[30] In other words, they possess a strong drive to analyze detail, and then discern the system that makes sense of the detail. Since their brains are hard-wired to do this type of analysis, those with AS often see relationships the rest of us miss.

For example, neuro-typical folks might walk into a coffee shop and comment that it feels comfortable. Someone with AS might notice that all of the round tables are placed in the center of the room and all of the square tables are arranged around the perimeter, and then notice that other "comfortable" coffee shops also share that configuration. From that, he might conclude that the arrangement of the tables plays a role in creating a comfortable setting in a coffee shop. This becomes an idea-link he can reapply elsewhere.

Since those with Asperger's are born with "their systemizing mechanism set on high," they're more apt to recognize systems and patterns. Over time, they'll come to possess more of these types of "pattern recognition" idea-links than the rest of us. Pattern and system recognition is "where" they are creative because that's where their interest is directed and that's what they analyze. So you see, they are creative, even though they score poorly on standardized creativity tests.

This means that if you've always told yourself you're not creative, or a creativity test told you the same, it's not true. You may not have analyzed as many subject areas as others, but in some area, in some part of your life where you have a deep level of interest and curiosity, you've dug in and manufactured idea-links. That makes you creative. More importantly, it proves you have the capacity to become more creative if you're willing to expand your curiosity into more areas, and undertake the analytical work needed to make more idea-links within those areas.

SIDETRACK: Hiring for Curiosity

Need a quick infusion of creativity into your organization? Find and hire new employees who already demonstrate innate curiosity. If you're wondering how to do that, ask Barry Wolfish.

As senior vice president of corporate marketing and communications for Land O'Lakes Inc., Wolfish hires marketers across a diverse set of businesses. A Land O'Lakes hire might market WinField™ Solutions seed and crop protection products and services, or Purina® animal nutrition products, or retail food brands such as LAND O LAKES® cheese and butter. The distinctive nature of each of these businesses would lead most hiring managers to look for specific backgrounds and interests to align with a specific business unit. Wolfish looks for something more: intellectual curiosity.

Why hire the intellectually curious? Over his three decades as a marketer and general manager, Wolfish noticed, "the marketers who approach life as generalists, who know a little bit about lots of things, are better at identifying the bigger opportunities, better at unleashing the bigger potential of the organization." Wolfish found those who are naturally curious remain curious about the inner workings of sales, manufacturing and distribution, and the consumers they serve, even though the organization may have internal specialists whose primary job is to understand and manage those same functional areas. "Because curious marketers see their jobs more broadly than just marketing, they see opportunities or obstacles across the business the less curious miss."

Wolfish also lauds these curious types for stimulating fresh thinking in the organization. "When they move into a new business unit, they can't help but ask questions; that's what curious people do. Their questions shake up the status quo and provoke new thinking."

So how does he find these curious types? Wolfish is the first to admit, he's no psychologist. But his nontraditional approach to interviewing, honed over the years, consistently yields the curious types he covets. His current hires tell me that an hour with Wolfish is the most unorthodox and interesting interview you'll ever experience. The first half delves into the usual interview stuff, such as past experiences and results. "The tip of the iceberg that's visible to any interviewer," as Wolfish puts it. To see what's underneath, Wolfish moves off-script.

"I have no formal plan for the second half of the interview. Eventually, I find out what interests them and how deeply they think about their interests or hobbies. If we get into a discussion about, say, Obama's new jobs plan, I want to know they've thought deeply about it, or at least asked themselves questions about the plan."

By moving beyond the typical interviewing drill, Wolfish uncovers more about the candidate. "Eventually, I see the whole person and how they think, including how curious they are. Often, what you discover about a person below the surface proves much more powerful than what's visible."

Think you could fool Wolfish by feigning interest or faking hobbies? Not likely, says the no-nonsense Wolfish, himself the curious type. "I'm a tenacious questioner. With enough questions, you eventually separate the curious from the less curious."

But knowing Wolfish's interviewing secret only gets you halfway toward matching his success. "If you're going to hire for curiosity," he warns, "you can't then place them in an environment that restricts their ability to explore. Or tell them, 'Here is the answer, do this.' If you do, you'll kill off the very creative spirit you're seeking to inject into your organization. Shut down their curiosity and the highly curious will actually underperform their less curious peers."

The Old Creativity

The more places you take
your curiosity, the more
creative you'll become.

You can't mandate
creativity.

The New Creativity

The more places you take
your curiosity, the more
creative you'll become
. . . when you create idea-
links in each place.

You can mandate the
time and the process to
build creativity.

5

Storing Idea-Links—Putting Your Work in the Bank

Everything has been thought of before; the problem is to think of it again.

—Johann Wolfgang von Goethe,
German philosopher

Once I was asked to pick three adjectives to describe creative people. While I struggled mightily to narrow the field down to three, it was a snap picking the first two: *inquisitive* and *acquisitive*. While you obviously know what these words mean, read the definitions below just for fun.

in·quis·i·tive

1. Given to inquiry, research, or asking questions; eager for knowledge; intellectually curious: **an inquisitive mind.**

2. Unduly or inappropriately curious; prying.

ac·quis·i·tive

1. Characterized by a strong desire to gain and possess.

2. Tending to acquire and retain ideas or information: **an acquisitive mind.**

What's surprising about both these definitions is the intensity of each word. Inquisitive people are more than just curious; they're curious nearly to the point of annoyance. They pry into everything. Think Jerry Seinfeld, spending an entire episode trying to figure out why his date won't eat apple pie. Or Hermione, retreating to the Hogwarts library again and again to satisfy her curiosity. That level of curiosity. When it comes to building your creativity, the speed of your growth is directly proportionate to the intensity of your inquisitiveness.

Inquisitiveness has an important and equally aggressive partner: acquisitiveness. Without an equally "strong desire to gain and possess" the idea-links you root out, the inquisitive act is an academic exercise. You have to find some way to make idea-links yours, to burn them in or save them, somewhere, for easy access later. To paraphrase Goethe, remembering them again is the problem.

Mentally Cataloging Idea-Links

The latest brain and memory research helps us find ways to better commit idea-links to memory. Anthony Greene is an associate professor of psychology at the University of Wisconsin in Milwaukee, where he runs a learning and memory lab. In the August 2010 issue of *Scientific American Mind*, Greene offers key insights about the recording and retrieval of memory.[31] Some of these we can use to improve how we record and retrieve idea-links. Among them:

1. **Memory springs from connections and associations.** We tend not to remember solitary facts as easily as those accompanied by a web of associations. For example, when we recall 9/11, we can't help but recall other aspects of that day. Where we were. What we were doing. Who we were with. When we see those people again, we can't help but associate 9/11 with them. My memory of 9/11 is forever linked with Sheila Burke, with whom I was meeting that morning. When I think of 9/11, I think of Sheila. When I think of Sheila, I think of 9/11. I'm sure she's not thrilled to be associated with such a tragic event, but that's how memory works.

2. **We remember things better when we put them in context.** Since memory springs from associations, it helps to remember the initial context as well—the story or situation from which it was extracted. For example, recalling the idea-link "people are motivated by feedback to save energy" is easier if I think about it in the context of my Prius research. If the idea-link is simply free-floating in your brain, it's likely to float away without a context to anchor it.

3. **We remember things we feel have some predictive value.** In other words, the brain places an emphasis on those items it feels will help us at some point in the future. If we see our friend enter a cave and get eaten by a bear, we see predictive value in remembering that caves sometimes contain bears and that bears always contain teeth. Hence, we never forget it.

4. **We remember better when we summarize key points and think about how we would teach or tell it to someone else.** Think about the difference between learning to do well on an exam, and learning something well enough to teach it. Information forced in through cramming is often lost soon after the exam because you don't really expect to need it later, or you figure you can always refer back to your book. If you learn a concept well enough to teach it, it tends to stay with you forever.

Knowing these facts about memory, I've developed an approach that helps you commit an idea-link to memory. Let's use the Prius again as an example.

Identification: First, you notice that a lot of people are buying Priuses in your neighborhood. Being curious, you want to understand what the hubbub is all about.

Analysis: Through investigation, analysis, or deep thinking, you discover that a big part of the Prius's appeal is the immediate feedback drivers receive from the dashboard instrumentation. This not only increases their enjoyment of the vehicle, it encourages them to save even more.

Prediction of Value: Next, you decide if this idea-link is memory-worthy. Is it interesting enough to hold potential future value? If you think it might be at all memory-worthy—for example, you're currently working on green initiatives at your company—acknowledge it accordingly. If not, consider letting it go, but discard it with caution. The most novel connections occur across seemingly unrelated areas, so err toward the side of inclusion. Future value is hard to predict when it comes to idea-links.

Summarization: Summarize mentally or on paper the idea-link you created through your analysis and note the story it originated from. For the feedback idea-link, it might look something like:

Immediate feedback is a powerful motivator to get people to change behavior (Prius).

or

Immediate feedback is a powerful motivator to get people to save energy (Prius).

Note that I placed the idea-link beside its origin (the Prius story). Remembering your idea-link with its originating story establishes context. Context in the form of story aids memory.

I encourage you to create a web of key linking words. Remember, when an idea-link comes up, it's usually because some association triggers it. The better the word associations you attach to your link, the better your chances it will come back when you need it to create an idea. Think of it like tagging a picture or a file with key words; the tags will help trigger access to the idea-link, the same way key words help you access a file. Depending on how you wrote the idea-link, here's how to highlight the key words—literally if you're writing it down, or figuratively if you're trying to commit it to memory.

> **Immediate feedback** is a powerful **motivator** to get people to **change behavior** (Prius).

> or

> **Immediate feedback** is a powerful **motivator** to get people to **save energy** (Prius).

Remembering the link in this way, you're setting it up to pop whenever you're working on a problem and someone mentions "changing behavior," "feedback," "motivation," or "saving energy." For example, when I created the hypothetical story about saving energy with home heating, the words "saving energy" immediately triggered the Prius idea-link for saving energy. Likewise, if a future problem involves motivation or getting people to change their behavior, I'm more likely to remember and apply my Prius idea-link if I've thought—even briefly—about the key words *motivation* and *change behavior.* If I'm working on a problem with childhood obesity and someone states that the real problem is *changing behavior,* my mind jumps to the Prius idea-link. From there, I begin to process how we might use immediate feedback to encourage kids to eat differently—for example, a wristwatch that shows how blood sugar spikes immediately after they drink a sugary soda.

While this process seems like a lot to remember in order to store an idea-link, the reality is you only need to practice it a few times before you get the drill down and it becomes natural. If I break down and list the steps of hitting a topspin forehand in tennis and you've never done it before, you might assume you could never learn to hit with topspin. At first blush, there are way too many steps to remember and there's far too little time to react. The ball sails past while you're still reading step two. But like learning topspin, the process of committing idea-links to memory becomes a reflex. Just as you can't expect to get better at tennis without learning new skills (e.g., hitting with topspin), you can't expect to get better at creativity without learning the process of mentally cataloging idea-links. The key is to move the behavior from explicit to implicit learning. According to Gonzales:

> When you learn something complex, such as flying, snowboarding, or tennis, at first you must think through each move. That's called explicit learning, and it's stored in explicit memory, the kind you can talk about, the kind that allows you to remember a recipe for lasagna. But as you gain more experience, you begin to do the task less consciously. You develop flow, touch, timing—a feel for it. It becomes second nature, a thing of beauty. That's known as implicit learning.[32]

The goal of this book isn't just to teach you about idea-links and how to make them. The goal is to teach you how to turn the process of recording idea-links into something you implicitly follow, so you're constantly developing your own creative raw material, almost without thought. But first you'll need to navigate the process and practice it with explicit memory—and that means deliberately going through the cataloging process until it becomes second nature.

The more disciplined you are about following a process to remember or record your idea-links, the more quickly you'll move from explicit learning to implicit learning. With implicit learning, the idea-link recording process becomes just part of how you naturally respond to the stimulus of seeing or hearing something interesting.

Physically Cataloging Idea-Links

Another storage option is to create a physical or virtual location for your links. This can be as easy as creating a physical file labeled "idea-links," then tossing in slips of paper as idea-links occur to you, or jotting down an idea-link on an article or print ad before placing it in the file. Or, you can take it a step further and create a spreadsheet with several columns (idea-link, origin, key words, etc.) so you can sort them by topic area and access them later.

Yet another option is to email idea-links to yourself, then drag them into an idea-link sub-folder within your email archive. From there, you can organize your idea-links however you want. Or record idea-links as voice memos on your smart phone and pick a day each month to convert them to text. (Also, check TheNewCreativity.com website. Someday I may have an app for that.)

You'll have to realistically assess your own organizational abilities and decide what works best for you, but whatever your method, keep two things in mind. First, give yourself freedom to experiment. You might start with a physical file then discover as it grows that you need a different system. Second, revisit your idea-links from time to time. Think back to Jack Gust's file of interesting things. By continually returning to his file, Gust ends up holding the idea-links in his filing cabinet and in his brain. Thus he's more creative wherever he goes, not just when he's near his filing cabinet.

Cataloging Idea-Links as a Group, Team, or Company

The physical cataloging process becomes a whole lot more powerful once you begin to think about teams, divisions, or entire companies. That's where technology can turn the idea-link gathering process from one individual trying to add links to his or her own memory, to an entire company building a physical asset base of creative raw material that can be repeatedly tapped for inspiration by everyone in the company.

In fact, using technology to collectively store and share idea-links is the single best way to overcome the vexing challenges of "too much focus on execution" and "not enough time to be creative" that we discussed in chapter four.

Arya Badiyan is a marketing director at Nestlé who leads a worldwide team for the Fitness cereal brand. Badiyan and the Fitness team created a website that serves as a collection place for all the insights and questions the team gathers. "We think of it as one big brain. When one of us gleans an insight, either from some research, a conversation with a customer, or a hunch in the middle of the night, we add it to the site. Other people look at it and make new connections."

> *. . . using technology to collectively store and share idea-links is the best way to overcome the challenge of "not enough time to be creative."*

What if your team or company could create its own "team brain" for the purpose of storing and sharing idea-links? Creating a virtual and ever-expanding gathering place for your idea-links is powerful for three reasons.

1. **A central gathering place allows you to move your idea-link quickly from working memory to long-term memory.** When you first hear something, unless it's emotionally charged, it stays in working memory until some other thought barges in and kicks it out. Since working memory is finite, it typically can't hold many thoughts at once. Unless something is successfully moved from working memory to long-term memory before another thought crowds it out, the idea-link is lost.[33] Since most of us are connected to the Internet during our waking hours, or have immediate access to it, storing idea-links in a web-based location helps ensure their survival.

2. **A central pool of idea-links builds the creativity of each individual much more quickly than having to create your own pool.** Think of the difference between having to forage for food on your own versus having hundreds of people sharing food at a central location. A collective site brings everyone's links to you and just scanning them makes you instantly more creative. But remember, everyone is responsible for adding idea-links, so do your part. And, when you're adding idea-links, don't be lazy—context matters. You may have to attach a short story along with your idea-link. Without context, the link may not make sense to someone else.

3. **Creating a central gathering point increases the odds that everyone will be motivated to look for idea-links.** Group pressure and group momentum are powerful motivators for most people. If a personal trainer says you need to start walking every day at lunchtime to lose weight, you might do it. If the trainer tells you that all your fellow employees are going and you'll all be sharing

the results of your weight loss efforts, you'll probably have greater motivation. Making idea-link-recording a team activity with a central site provides the same type of motivation.

Make the Method Match Your Needs

The type of idea-links you need to store and how you plan to use them to inspire yourself (or others) should drive the way you store them. I convert mine to laminated cards because during my ideations I need others to pass them around and react to them. The need for portability and durability drives my storage method. There's no single best way; think it through and be open to creative approaches. Take 3M for example.

At the core of 3M's culture of innovation is perhaps the world's greatest collection of technologies and techno-logical capabilities, which are continually expanded upon by the scientists who work there. Perhaps just as important as expanding into new technologies, is expanding the existing technologies into new places. Employees in all functions are encouraged to continually transfer these technologies to new markets, new products, and new users in new and different ways.

3M recognizes that these technologies can only be reconnected to new places if employees and customers understand how the technologies work and what they're capable of doing. In other words, they must see and under-stand the essence of the technology to reapply it elsewhere. Extracting the essence of each technology is another way of saying you're extracting its idea-link so it can be recon-nected over and over. The technology itself is the fact; the idea-link is the deep understanding of how it really works at its most basic level. That's the piece that's connectable.

To draw inspiration from 3M's multitude of technologies, this understanding must become second nature; 3M employees must become one with the technologies, much like Paul Simon relies on his catalog of sounds. So when 3M thought about how to "store" technologies, they conceived a storage method that allows employees to fully immerse themselves in each technology. They don't just learn how each technology works; they experience how it works.

If you're lucky enough to someday enter 3M's gleaming new Innovation Center you'll see what I mean. The center is an ever-expanding, highly interactive shrine to technological innovation. Each technology station explains and demonstrates not only how the technology works and how it's currently applied, but also how it might be combined with other technologies to solve problems. Mix in customers with real needs, and the Innovation Center buzzes with creative energy. As 3M employees and their customers collaboratively interact with these stations, they make startling new connections among 3M's capabilities and the customers' needs, both articulated and unarticulated.

Regardless of how you want to capture your idea-links, the point is that you need some system in place, whether it's mastery of the memorization method, or creating a physical or virtual space for storage. Inquisitiveness—the curiosity-driven analysis that creates idea-links—is only the starting point. Only by acquiring them—actually storing the links for future access—can you fully tap their creative value.

• • •

As we leave chapter five, we are about to enter a new stage of Discipline 1—taking your understanding of idea-link making and applying it directly and specifically to your job. Before we do, take a moment to burn in your new mantra:

Notice. Analyze. Store.

Notice. Analyze. Store.

Notice. Analyze. Store.

This is our foundation. Simply noticing the world around you, analyzing how and why things work, and then storing the resulting idea-links will make you more creative. Notice. Analyze. Store.

With that foundation in place, we can build. From this point on we get heavily into the application mode, so you'll need full attention to the task. If you've read nonstop to this point, rest your brain. Let things digest a bit. And then get out your highlighter, electronic or otherwise, as we move from noticing the idea-links that might help you someday, to deliberately finding the idea-links that can help you right now.

The Old Creativity	The New Creativity
Individuals keep creative assets in their heads.	Individuals create and share creative assets as a team.
Creative assets die when people leave.	Creative assets grow with the company.

6

Finding Idea-Links for Important Subject Areas

Thanks to their naturally high curiosity levels, highly creative people instinctively create idea-links. Even though you may not have been born with the same level of curiosity as a highly creative person, once you understand how creativity is built, it's a process everyone can mimic. If you take your newfound ability and focus it on your career or on a specific project, you accelerate your ability to be creative in a particular job function, or in solving a particular problem. In the next two chapters, we'll do just that.

As you read through the next two chapters, have in mind your own profession or a current problem you're working on. Take what you learn from the examples and think about how you might apply it to your own situation. By doing so, you'll make the idea-link creation process immediately relevant to your life and to your success, which will go a long way toward encouraging you to continue. And that's my ultimate goal—to get you started and keep you going on your journey toward becoming more creative.

Finding Your Focus

Let's look at creativity in the context of innovation. Innovation is the process of generating an idea, and bringing the idea to fruition. The innovation can be a new product, a new company, or simply a new way of doing things. Innovations can be big or small, breakthrough or incremental.

Creativity is a skill that is applied throughout the process of innovation. You might use creativity to come up with a new product idea, or a new way to get around barriers to execution, or a creative way to speed up a process. In each case, you're using creativity to advance innovation.

If creativity is a skill, in what subject area do you want to build that skill? Specifically, in what subject area are you continually asked to come up with creative ideas? That's where you should focus your attention. That's where you'll build your library of idea-links.

So far, I've shown you random idea-links in everything from music to design to entertainment to marketing. Every subject area is ripe for its own collection of idea-links, whether it's something broad like Cost-Saving Idea-Links or Growth Idea-Links, or narrowly focused on your core business like Fast-Food Restaurant Success Idea-Links. Define your subject area, then start digging and collecting.

TRIZ: Engineering's Idea-Link Library

If your profession is engineering, someone already did some heavy digging for you—and over a half-century ago. That's when a Russian man named Genrich Altshuller created something known as The Theory of Inventive Problem Solving, or TRIZ (pronounced *treez*). In the late 1940s, Altshuller was a patent investigator for the Russian Navy. Being the ambitious sort, Altshuller aspired to be more than just a glorified clerk; he wanted to get in the game himself. He wondered if he could help patent-seeking inventors overcome some of their technical problems by adding his own creative solutions. But first, he needed to become more creative himself. Altshuller started by studying the behavior of the applicants. If he did what they did, he reasoned, he might become more creative. However, he only hit pay dirt when he moved his focus away from the applicants and started sifting through the patent applications themselves. Altshuller's discovery? The creative value wasn't in understanding what made the inventors succeed, but rather in understanding what made the inventions succeed.

As a patent investigator, Altshuller had thousands of case studies to draw upon in the form of patent applications. By closely studying the applications, instead of the applicants, Altshuller noticed patterns, particularly in the most innovative patents. These applications followed a predictable flow to solve various engineering problems. As a result of his analysis, this patent investigator turned aha-moment identifier discovered forty such principles of identifiable ingenuity. These became the basis for TRIZ.

The forty TRIZ principles carry intimidating, engineer-loving names like "equipotentiality" (instead of raising your car to change your oil, you simply stick some dude in a pit and park over him) and "spheroidality" (think of the ball inside your mouse, or replacing the four fixed wheels on your vacuum cleaner with a ball, as Dyson has done, for greater maneuverability).[34] In our lingo, they're simply idea-links. And in the engineering world, they're golden.

An entire industry developed around these TRIZ principles, and now engineers around the world use them to make new connections. In fact, any of us could've invented the much-heralded Dyson vacuum cleaner that turns on a ball instead of on four fixed wheels by mentally going through each TRIZ principle, one by one. Eventually, we would land on spheroidality, which would tell us to think about replacing four fixed wheels with one big one and we would say, "Aha," just like the hotshots at Dyson.

As Altshuller put it, "You could wait a hundred years for enlightenment, or you can solve the problem in fifteen minutes with these principles."[35] That's true in engineering; it can be true in your field as well.

Making This Chapter Work for You

What about your area of expertise? What if you work in marketing or promotions or PR or finance or manufacturing? Or education? Or sales? Or human resources? Or in a technical field? Would you rather be like the engineer who knows about and has access to TRIZ, or the one who doesn't?

Shouldn't every discipline, every subject, every job function have its own batch of idea-links, just as engineering has TRIZ? What would you look at and analyze in your field? In demonstrating how I might gather idea-links in certain subject areas, my intent is to trigger ideas for how you might gather them in the fields important to you. Thinking about your own job functions as you read through the process and examples will help you figure it out, even if some of the areas covered are far from your profession.

Making This Chapter Work for Your Company

You can think about the gathering of idea-links within a subject area as an individual exercise, a group project, or even a company-wide mission. For example, General Mills's stated goal is to become the best branding company in the world. Not just within the food industry, but the best branding company, period. With a stable of brand power-houses like Yoplait, Cheerios, Wheaties, Green Giant, and Nature Valley, to name just a few, they've certainly got the assets to work with. But saying you want to be the most creative branding company in the world and doing the work to make it happen are two different things.

Enter Mark Addicks, General Mills's chief marketing officer and truly one of the world's most creative marketers. Addicks has always been a sponge for brand stories, with an almost encyclopedic recall for the details. Mention a brand, any brand, and he'll likely have a story at the ready. Give him a branding challenge, and he'll have a creative solution nearly as fast.

In 2001, Addicks developed Brand Champions, a week-long training program for all General Mills Inc. (GMI) marketers to learn branding from some of the best in the company. More interestingly, Brand Champions exposes marketers to over 250 cases of branding excellence outside of General Mills. You'd think 250 cases would do the trick, but not for Addicks. His team emails monthly branding case studies to GMI marketers around the globe. These highly entertaining and easily accessible narratives, along with various other internal and external examples, have added another 200 cases to the collective mental library. Want your company to become more creative at branding than General Mills? You're 450 cases behind and the gap is widening every month.

Regardless of whether you plan on using these idea-links personally or company-wide, the impact is the same: Those who possess more idea-links will be more creative in their chosen areas than those who possess fewer.

Positioning Idea-Links

Positioning is a concept most often associated with marketers and advertisers, but it's a necessary skill for anyone who needs to sell an idea or product. Whether you're trying to persuade junior-high students to stay off drugs or convince your boss you deserve a promotion, finding the one best way to communicate your idea will often make or break it.

One of my favorite positioning stories comes courtesy of Barry Feig, a new product consultant in New Mexico. In his book, *Marketing Straight to the Heart*, Feig tells the story of positioning a new Glad-Lock storage bag, the first one with a color seal that tells you if the bag is sealed tight. The idea of a blue side meeting a yellow side to create a green strip to indicate a securely sealed bag seems like an obviously good idea in hindsight. But the women in Feig's focus groups didn't think so; they complained that the idea insulted them. They didn't need help closing a bag!

Undaunted, Feig returned with a new positioning statement. "What if we said, 'It's so easy to close properly, even your husband and kids can get it right?'" They thought that was a great idea, and went on to explain in detail all the times their dim-bagging husbands ruined expensive food, or how their crazy kids leaked bags of bright red Kool-Aid into the deep recesses of the family fridge. Same product, but a different positioning made all the difference.[36]

I read Feig's book and remembered his story. More importantly, I filed away the positioning idea-link: **Sometimes you can make a product so simple or convenient you might actually insult the buyer. In these cases, shift your attention to a third party who's a user, but not the buyer (Glad-Lock bags).**

Sure enough, two years later I'm working with a cheese company. We complete the ideation work, and then develop a batch of rough concepts for consumer feedback. I agree to moderate the focus groups. Among the many concepts is this one: a presliced block of cheese. Not cubes in a bag, but a block of cheese that's presliced and still in the block shape (like a loaf of sliced bread). We thought female shoppers would love the added convenience. Guess what happened? They hated it. "What do you think, we don't know how to cut cheese?" we heard from our first focus group in suburban Detroit.

Holding back the obvious but inappropriate "cheese-cutting" comeback, I retreated to the back room to confer with the marketing manager. "What the hell happened?" he wondered. "I can't believe they hate it."

"We can save it," I assured him, and headed back to the piranha tank. "Okay, what if we said 'Here is a product that's already cut for you; it makes removing a slice of cheese so easy that even your husbands and kids can do it right?'"

Instantly, they changed their tune. "Oh my God! My husband breaks off a piece of cheese like he's some kind of starving caveman—he destroys it every time. And don't get me started on my kids and knives—I'm scared to death they'll end up with half their thumb on top of a Triscuit." Stories of their families' cheese-cutting futility went on and on.

While the concept never scored well enough in concept tests to warrant introduction (turns out it wasn't the greatest thing since sliced bread), in that moment I was a hero in my client's eyes—all because I had filed away Feig's positioning story for future use. Positioning idea-links are like that. The same one can often be used across multiple categories.

Don't just remember the ad; remember why it worked

When you're positioning a new concept of any kind, you're looking for inspiration. What possible angles can we use to motivate people to buy or accept this idea? What insights can we leverage? While there are many techniques you can apply to arrive at the answers to these questions, one you should consider is looking through a catalog of positioning angles successfully used by others. In essence, create your own book of positioning idea-links. I've collected lots of these over the years because positioning is an area in which I need to be continually creative. And you can bet that a brain jam-packed with positioning idea-links (and their related backstories) beats a brain with just a few rattling around. Every time. Guaranteed.

The good news is that positioning links are super easy to find. That's because most successful products, services, companies, or politicians (especially politicians) have at their core a successful positioning strategy that got them there in the first place. All you have to do is pay attention to the *why*.

Whenever you see a print ad, billboard, blog, viral video, television spot, or home page that comes across as exceedingly clear or especially motivating, stop and study it. Not later; you'll forget. What was the message? What was the underlying insight? How did they make it memorable? How did they differentiate themselves from the rest of the market? Why did it resonate? Why did it motivate? The answer to one of these questions will result in an idea-link. File these positioning links away, because one might spring forth later and land you in the executive wing.

One example: A recent Dodge Charger ad struck me, not because it was particularly motivating to me at my stage in life, but I could see how it could be to others. In it, a series of thirty-something husbands stare into the camera and deliver compliant, whipped-puppy lines such as:

"I will get up and walk the dog at 6:30 am."

"I will eat some fruit as part of my breakfast."

"I will clean the sink after I shave."

"I will listen to your opinions of my friends."

"I will listen to your friends' opinions of my friends."

"I will be civil to your mother."

"I will remember to put the seat down."

This goes on for some time, until the payoff: ". . . and because I do this, I will drive the car I want to drive. Dodge Charger. Man's. Last. Stand."

If you search for the ad online, you'll probably react as most do: "That's a great ad." But stopping there doesn't give you a positioning idea-link. There is no creative potential in knowing it's a great ad. What was the truth behind the spot that made it compelling? What was the insight?

You can probably assume the agency or client behind the spot discovered there were two main categories of potential buyers: Men who got the car they wanted regardless of how strongly their wives protested, and men who really wanted to buy a muscle car like a Charger, but were worried (or afraid) their wives would deem it impractical and put the kibosh on it. The spot clearly targets the latter. But how does the spot overcome such a barrier? By appealing to the male need to feel, well, male. By appealing to the male desire to express, "Enough is enough, I get my say on *something* and this is the thing." This positioning approach doesn't attempt to make them want the car more. It just plants in them the internal rationale (or courage) to push it further with their spouse.

So here's the idea-link: **One way to position a product for men is to appeal to their need to feel "manly" and "in control" when it comes to making purchase decisions (Charger ad).**

By remembering it in the context of the Charger ad, you'll recall that this positioning works especially well when males share the decision process with their mates—and it works especially well if their mates may not be thrilled by the purchase.

To see another example of the same usage, Google "Flo TV ad Jim Nantz" to see an ad featuring a payoff line that will stick in my mind forever: "Change out of that skirt, Jason." Once you're aware of this idea-link, you'll start to see it in many of the products that target men.

By the way, for the women reading this with amusement (or disgust) for how easily men are manipulated, or for how manipulating marketers can be, don't get too smug. You, too, fall victim to the evil clutches of marketers who know how to bend your psyche to their will. One is called the "you deserve it" positioning—it's marketers' way of helping you feel better about buying everything from high-calorie white-chocolate mochas to exotic spa treatments. Your rational brain knows you can't afford the extra calories or the expensive treatment, but your emotional brain says, "Dammit, they're right—I do deserve it!"

Next time you watch TV, or drive to work, try to pick up at least one positioning link from the ads you encounter. Do this each day and before long, you won't be able to stop yourself. Then, once you've gathered twenty or so positioning links (and hopefully a new promotion), treat yourself to a deliciously decadent caramel mocha frappuccino from Starbucks. Go ahead, you deserve it!

New Product Idea-Links

Back in the 1990s when I taught a New-Product Marketing course to MBA students, I started each class with a fifteen-minute segment called "This Week in New

Products." The idea was simple. Each week, students were to scout for new product introductions and arrive prepared to discuss why they thought the new product, service, or company would succeed or fail. Likewise, their final paper consisted of finding an existing success or failure and analyzing all the principles behind its success or failure. At the time I didn't realize it, but both assignments forced students to create idea-links—a term I had yet to coin.

If a major part of your job revolves around new products, there are two places to look for new-product idea-links: Those inside your current categories or channels, and those outside your current categories and channels. While knowing that doesn't narrow the field, it's important to make the distinction anyway because each resource leads to different kinds of ideas.

Looking inside your category

Those idea-links inside your category or industry typically represent success factors—these are the links that generally improve your likelihood of success. They're proven formulas that can be reapplied or reconnected in different ways over and over. A good example is the *Idol* formula, which was successfully reapplied within entertainment to shows featuring modeling, dancing, fashion design, and cooking. All are new ideas, but each employs a proven TV formula. It has just been reapplied to a new skill to create a new show. Can creating a new show in this way be called an act of creativity? Sure—just because it's easy and obvious doesn't make its creation any less valuable.

Many new products simply reapply idea-links from within their category. While it may not be the sexiest way to create new ideas, to ignore them is folly. We might call new ideas created this way a rip-off, but they're smart rip-offs, and most successful new products, even in your industry, fit this classification.

Banana Nut Crunch cereal and Cinnamon Toast Crunch cereal taste nothing alike, yet they spring from the same idea-link: **Create new cereals based on well-known food analogs.** Similarly, when Vytorin successfully entered the cholesterol-lowering medicine fray with their "treats the two sources of cholesterol" (food and family) positioning, a raft of new medications followed for other conditions, each promising to treat two *sources* of whatever ailment they targeted—or lately, two concurrent *ailments* or *conditions* at the same time. This type of thinking isn't lazy; it's efficient.

Before you start jumping on these intra-category success factors, I'll offer one warning: You can't just apply them willy-nilly. You still have to think.

If you develop new cars or new car designs for a living, you may fully understand from your Prius analysis that many buyers of hybrid vehicles want to make their hybrid ownership visible to others to make a social statement. Reapplying this idea-link probably directed the designers of the Tahoe Hybrid to plaster a giant HYBRID sticker that spans the entire side of the vehicle. But will the same consumers who want to wear their vehicle as an outward symbol of their greenness choose to express it with a 5,688-pound gas-electric land barge? Will it scream, "Look at me, I'm green!" or will it cynically whisper, "Here comes the hypocrite"? Creatively reapplying idea-links from within your own category improves your chances of success, but it doesn't guarantee it.

Looking outside your category

Looking *outside* (or adjacent to) your categories and channels gives you idea-links that can lead to more novel thinking—the kinds of ideas that sometimes make sense only in hindsight. For example, think about the navigation devices from Garmin, TomTom, and others that allow you to download voices ranging from Darth Vader to Homer Simpson. If you want to become a great new-product person, when you see an idea like this outside your category—especially if you think it's a good idea—you should immediately think about how to apply it to your own category. That's what the most creative new-product people do automatically. More often than not, they come up with nothing. But every once in a while . . .

Let's pretend you're in charge of creating new options for Ford or GM vehicles and you've just read about the downloadable *Star Wars* and *The Simpsons* GPS voices in the adjacent car accessories category. By now, you know that idea-link making isn't about taking the idea literally. I'm not telling you to build a Darth Vader–edition Ford Focus or a Chevy Bart-mobile, but rather to think about what the new GPS feature really offers: **Use simple download technology so consumers can customize a product to their liking (Simpsons GPS voice).**

Now that we have the idea in its linkable form, we can let our minds run with it. First, let's stay close to the original idea-link and think specifically about customization of sound. Again, we're pretending we work for a car manufacturer who needs to come up with new vehicle options. What sounds does a car make and which could be customized? Well, how about the horn? If you can choose your GPS voice, why can't you choose and download a "voice" for the horn?

We have our own ringtones, but we're pretty much stuck with the sound of the horn that comes with the car. Granted, we can't go crazy on this one. We'll certainly encounter regulatory restrictions that will keep customized car horns from playing the chorus of Cee Lo Green's "Forget You." But there are thousands of sounds that will do the same job as current horns and still allow drivers to express their individuality. That's just one idea.

Here's another idea that springs from the same idea-link—why can't a horn make multiple sounds? Why don't cars have a friendly honk sound to go along with the "I'm-mad-as-hell" honk? When someone is courteous enough to let us in as we leave a concert, we give them the same honk we offer the jerk who cuts us off on the way to the concert. When it comes to horns, all we know how to do is shake our fist; we can't honk a message that says, "Thank you, kind soul, for letting me out of this lane that never moves and away from the guy with the I'd Rather Be Sailing bumper sticker who probably should be sailing instead of driving." Thinking about the new product idea-link behind the *Star Wars* GPS voice—an idea outside the category of auto manufacturing—leads to the idea of a novel new car feature: The friendly horn.

Now let's isolate the customization portion of the TomTom idea-link and apply it to the car industry, forgetting about sounds. What other elements of a vehicle are you stuck with from the time you buy it until you sell it? What items can never be changed or customized? Which of those elements might be fun to change or modify? What about a variety of snap-on, snap-off grills? Grills, more than any other element, establish the personality of the vehicle. They literally are the expression on your car's face. And I'm guessing there are people who'd pay good money to change theirs, perhaps daily. Or perhaps turn a dial to customize the color of your dash lights? Or the bings and beeps you hear when you open a door or forget to wear your seatbelts? We've been customizing sounds and colors for more than a decade in our computers and phones, why not in our cars?

The point with all these examples isn't whether these are desirable new-product features. The point is that generating these novel ideas is as simple as finding idea-links outside of your area and reapplying them inside it. Giving people different voices for their Garmin is the same as giving them different ringtones for their phone, which is the same as giving them different horns for their car, which is similar to giving them different grills for the front of their car.

Once you know what to look for, you'll find new product idea-links everywhere.

Publicity Idea-Links

If you're looking for ways to improve your brand or your company's awareness, there's no better method than publicity—it's much less expensive than advertising, and as long as you respect the source, it's also more credible. Here's an example of free publicity from an article I read on the internet in 2008.[37] If you Google "KFC Secret Recipe Moved," you'll find hundreds more just like it.

> Col. Harland Sanders's handwritten recipe of 11 herbs and spices was removed Tuesday from safekeeping at KFC's corporate offices for the first time in decades. The temporary relocation is allowing KFC to revamp security around a yellowing sheet of paper that contains one of the country's most famous corporate secrets.

The brand's top executive admitted his nerves were aflutter despite the tight security he lined up for the operation. "I don't want to be the president who loses the recipe," KFC President Roger Eaton said. "Imagine how terrifying that would be."

The recipe that launched the chicken chain was placed in a lock box that was handcuffed to security expert Bo Dietl, who climbed aboard an armored car that whisked away with an escort from off-duty police officers. Eaton's parting words to Dietl: "Keep it safe."

So important is the 68-year-old concoction that coats the chain's Original Recipe chicken that only two company executives at any time have access to it. The company refuses to release their names or titles, and it uses multiple suppliers who produce and blend the ingredients but know only a part of the entire contents.

The recipe has been stashed at the company headquarters for decades, and for more than 20 years has been tucked away in a filing cabinet equipped with two combination locks. To reach the cabinet, the keepers of the recipe would first open up a vault and unlock three locks on a door that stood in front of the cabinet. Vials of the herbs and spices are also stored in the secret filing cabinet.

Others have tried to replicate the recipe, and occasionally someone claims to have found a copy of Sanders's creation. The executive said none have come close, adding the actual recipe would include some surprises. Sanders developed the formula in 1940 at his tiny restaurant in southeastern Kentucky and used it to launch the KFC chain in the early 1950s.

Larry Miller, a restaurant analyst with RBC Capital Markets, said the recipe's value is "almost an immeasurable thing. It's part of that important brand image that helps differentiate the KFC product."

If part of your job is creating publicity or buzz, whenever you hear something that makes news you need to uncover the underlying principle that makes the story newsworthy. And by newsworthy I mean not just get-on-the-evening-news kind of news, but also news that's worthy of getting passed around the office, or from mom-to-mom, or from teen-to-teen.

So what was newsworthy about the KFC secret recipe in the first place, even before they moved it to a more secure location? Well, people love secrets. Some people like creating or containing secrets; others revel in discovering, revealing, or ruining them.

Does our obsession with secrets date back to more primitive times when news of a secret stash of acorns meant the difference between survival and death? It doesn't really matter. Secrets, properly crafted, make news and always have. This article and the success of the KFC brand prove it. So now you have one idea-link for building word of mouth or publicity: **Create, contain, or reveal a secret (KFC).** When you see a news story like one about KFC, take time to think about your own company or product. Is there some secret you can publicize, or if you don't have one, can you create one? Most companies and products do indeed have secrets, they just don't think of them as secrets—we call them our processes or methods or approaches or corporate principles. Putting the "secret" spin on the things you're currently doing, or the stuff you currently have, can turn the mundane into news.

Now, what if your entire team did nothing but pay attention to outside examples of publicity, then analyze why they work and extract idea-links, just as I've done here? You would create the TRIZ of publicity. What if next time you need to create buzz for your product, instead of feeling the typical back-against-the-wall kind of creative pressure, you simply peruse your list of two hundred publicity idea-links until one triggers a great new idea? What if you came up with a great new idea and you ran to your boss and said, "I have this great idea; it's kind of like what KFC did only different . . ."? At that moment, you'll have harnessed the true power of idea-links. And your boss will praise your creativity.

Digging deeper into news stories

When you find a news story that generates publicity, or a video that goes viral, leave open the possibility that there might be multiple reasons behind its success. Yes, in the case of KFC, there are even more idea-links inside this bucket of chicken. If you think about what made KFC newsworthy in the first place, it wasn't just the secret recipe, but the fact that it was *someone's* secret recipe, the iconic Colonel Sanders— long gone, but still peddling chicken in effigy form. Founders (and inventors) make good news stories. Steve Jobs of Apple. Dave Thomas of Wendy's. Art Fry of Post-it® Notes fame. Is there a hero story behind your next new-product introduction? An interesting character who makes it more than just a standard press release? Maybe you can't use it now, but for those of you who are in charge of generating publicity for your company, it's a link worth filing away: **Quote, profile, introduce, or create a company hero (Colonel Sanders).**

Now that we've pulled a few idea-links from KFC, let's start your list of publicity idea-links, using some from the Starbucks closed-for-training story in chapter four as well.

Publicity Idea-Links Master List (so far)

Create, maintain, or reveal a secret (KFC recipe, Coca-Cola formula).

Create a hero story or elevate the profile of an inventor, interesting character, customer, or CEO (Colonel Sanders, Steve Jobs, Dave Thomas, Art Fry, Jared of Subway).

Coordinate masses of people or employees (Starbucks training).

Do something that will hurt your business to prove a point (Starbucks training).

Let's add one more publicity idea-link—from a recent article in the business section of my local paper. The headline: "Build Your Own Corvette Engine." In a first for the industry, General Motors had the idea to give buyers who order a 2011 Corvette Z06 or ZR1 the chance to help assemble their car's high-performance engine at the factory. As part of the program, buyers take six hours to assemble their engines from the provided parts, while a skilled technician supervises the operation.[38]

You might figure the buyer *saves* money by assembling his own engine, right? Wrong. Buyers pay an additional $5,800 to feel a deeper connection to their new vehicle, which has a price tag starting at $75,000 and going as high as $100,000, depending on added features. And they pay their own airfare. But they do get a free night's stay in Wixom, a Detroit suburb.

Before I give you the publicity idea-link, think about how you'd write it, and you can compare our results.

Here's how I would remember it: **Involve buyers in the development or construction of a product or service with high emotional attachment (Corvette—build your own engine).**

Add it—however you expressed it—to your master list. Expand your list to two hundred publicity idea-links and each year you'll save your staff days in idea-generation time and get better ideas in the process.

Finance or Business Model Idea-Links

The most creative finance person I ever worked with never worked in finance; in fact, he knows little about it. But what he does know allows him to creatively construct new business models for the new ventures he leads. Bob Wolf is the head of advanced technology at Andersen Windows, the world's largest branded window manufacturer. A chemical engineer by training, Wolf holds sixteen patents from his prior work at 3M, including the gel-filled ergonomic wrist rest for keyboards. Like many of the creative people I work with, Wolf is an avid reader who's constantly poaching idea-links from a wide variety of books.

Some years ago when Bob was still at 3M, we worked together on a project with few boundaries. We knew the consumer need, but how we would answer it was entirely open, including what business model we would use to make money. Unbelievable creativity emerged out of this ambiguity, mostly thanks to Bob. As different ideas took shape, Bob would immediately offer different business models to organize around. Or, he would hybridize two business models into an altogether new one. Or he would start with a business model, and then fill in the idea around the model.

Astounded by how a chemical engineering major could generate so many different financial models, I asked his secret. As it turns out, Wolf had simply done what all the other creative geniuses did—he'd prepared his mind ahead of time.

Wolf had purchased the book *The Profit Zone*[39] in preparation for the project, read it, and then mentally acquired it. He went beyond highlighting; he cut and pasted the summaries of all twenty-two business models described in the book into one document—each summary long enough to get the gist of the business model, but short enough to commit to memory. (Business models are a type of idea-link because they succinctly explain how or why a certain kind of business creates, delivers, or captures value.) These twenty-two summarizing snippets formed the foundation for Wolf's creativity around financial business models. These twenty-two idea-links are available to anyone willing to put in the time to acquire them.

Finance is a broad field, so the type of finance idea-links you collect will no doubt vary with the type of finance job you hold. If you support an innovation group, filing away different business models will make you invaluable to the team. Even though *The Profit Zone* already exists as a TRIZ-like summary of fundamental business models, it still behooves you to analyze different business types—movies, clothing, casinos, automobiles—and make mental notes of winning aspects of their business models. New business model idea-links continually crop up, but you'll need to find them. What if you applied Costco's "treasure hunt" model to your business? Or the "deal-conceding buying power" of Groupon? Or the "pay what you want" strategy pioneered by Radiohead? If you're not familiar with how any of these work, you should stop reading now and Google them. Remember, the process of getting more creative is now in your hands and sometimes you need to get those hands dirty. The more you dig in and understand how each type of business ticks, the more creative you become in creating new business models for your own company.

Every finance job is different. Think about your job. Think about what Wolf did. Then determine what kind of idea-links would make you more creative in finance, Bob Wolf–style.

Cost-Saving Idea-Links

From the low-cost shingles on our homes, to the discount shoes on our feet, to the self-checkout kiosk at the grocery store, we're surrounded by cost-saving idea-links. Every time someone makes a less expensive item or finds a way to drive cost out of a product, operation, or process, there is a principle behind how they made it happen. Cost savings should have its own TRIZ and I bet if you put some of your smartest people on it, you could create one for your company. Here's how to start.

First, have someone catalog all the major cost-savings successes your organization has created over the past ten years, or as far back as you have records or historical knowledge. For each cost-saving success, take a cue from Wolf and his business-model summaries. Write down your example and then extract the principle behind it. Then put them somewhere you can readily access and add to them over time. If your company once saved money on a product by blending in 10% more of a less expensive ingredient (without negatively impacting product performance) then your idea-link is called something like: **Low-level blending: replace some of the original material with a lower-cost ingredient in an amount small enough to not compromise product integrity.**

Or, perhaps you figured out how to save on ingredient costs by increasing the intensity or efficacy of an ingredient, which is one of the primary reasons food companies use MSG (it intensifies flavor, which allows them to use less spice). The idea-link then is: **Add an ingredient that improves performance and allows us to use less of other ingredients.** If shingles are the product, this might mean finding a better performing adhesive so roofers can use fewer nails, under the premise that glue costs less than steel.

After you create your internal list, turn your cost-saving idea-linking team loose on the outside world. Unfortunately, the details of some cost-saving successes aren't readily shared with outsiders, so you may have to do some bartering. Offer your list of idea-links and idea-link stories to another company and ask if they can create the same for you. If you're going to companies who aren't competitors, they should do so readily—especially if you've both read this book.

Assign team members to different companies, or to entire categories in your search for inspiration. The cost-saving idea-links you collect become a sort of creative currency, each capable of unlocking millions of dollars in cost savings. But unlike traditional currency, idea-links carry unknown value. One idea-link can save millions of dollars a year if it leads to a great idea, whereas many others may never lead to anything tangible and thus never deliver any practical value to your company. Yet, one company's "useless" idea-link might unlock a big idea for a different company. Idea-link currency is like that—at the time you add a link to your collection, you won't know what it's worth. But you can generally assume that the more links you have, the greater the overall value of your stash.

Consumer-Insight Idea-Links

Talk to any seasoned marketers, market researchers, or advertisers and they'll tell you it's all about finding consumer insights. Winning ad ideas, brilliant marketing strategies, effective selling approaches, smart package redesign, and successful new products—all spring from consumer insights, or customer insights as they're called in the business-to-business world. In reality consumer insights are important to any profession.

So what exactly is a consumer insight? A consumer insight is a certain type of idea-link that comes from understanding why people do what they do, buy what they buy, or feel what they feel. And in the currency of idea-links, consumer insights are gem-like. You dig for insights the same way you dig for any idea-link: You seek to understand at a deeper level. You analyze. You ask probing questions. You separate the *why* from the *what*.

Anthropologists: the world's why diggers

Robbie Blinkoff is the Principal Anthropologist and Managing Director of Context-Based Research Group, a Baltimore-based firm specializing in ethnographic research. Ethnographers get to do all kinds of fun stuff like hang out in convenience stores and find out why, each day, twenty-something males guzzle their weight in energy drinks. Or they analyze videotapes of someone's morning grooming ritual to discover why they switch shampoos every third day. If you're wondering how you could be persuaded to let a complete stranger videotape you taking a shower, or shaving, or worse, ask Blinkoff. Somehow he and others like him figure out a way to record you in your skivvies.

Regardless of their methods, the researcher's goal is always the same. According to Blinkoff, "The reason to do ethnography is to gain an anthropological perspective on your customers—to get to the 'deep structure' behind why they do what they do. Above the surface, anthropologists observe people's behavior, the products and services they use, their thoughts. Think about these elements as the tree's trunk, limbs, and leaves. From observations, anthropologists generate insights into the underlying philosophies, motivations, and cultural foundations for why people do what they do. This part is below the surface—the tree's roots."

Another way to think about the tree's roots is to give them another name. Yep, idea-links. When you understand people's "true motivations, underlying philosophies and cultural foundations," you possess an incredible wealth of links that can lead you to ideas in practically any field, especially areas like marketing, sales, advertising, public relations, promotions, and communications. Really, any job that involves people—such as teaching, or law, or human resources—is performed more creatively when you understand what drives people's behavior.

You don't have to become a professional anthropologist like Blinkoff to uncover consumer-insight idea-links. In most cases, it requires nothing more than learning the art of the follow-up question to dig down to the roots.

See a behavior you find odd? Want to know why your friend, strapped by credit card debt, just purchased an expensive new purse? Just ask and you'll be amazed what you unearth. Remember to do so in the spirit of curiosity—do it in a judging manner and you'll likely to get the wrong answer, no answer, or worse, that expensive purse upside your head.

Ask an extra question (or two or three)

The "Take Me Fishing" ad campaign is one of the most effective and memorable advertising campaigns in the last decade. If you haven't seen it, I'll recreate it for you (or you can Google it and watch it now).[40] I'll warn you, though, if you're a dad with a daughter (like me), get your hanky ready. The narrator makes a highly emotional appeal to parents (especially fathers) to take their kids (especially their daughters) fishing. The fifteen-second ad copy goes like this:

> Take me fishing, because I get the giggles when the boat bounces.
>
> Take me fishing, you can think about work later.
>
> Take me fishing, because my wedding will be sooner than you think.

The last line is accompanied with an image of a young daughter, about the age of my daughter, gazing contentedly from one end of the boat while her dad fishes from the other.

"Take me fishing, because my wedding will be sooner than you think." Take Me Fishing™ National Campaign. ©RBFF, 2008.

In just fifteen seconds of words and images I'm welling up with tears. No way my daughter is getting married before she gets her time with Dad! That's one regret I can't live with! Within days, I plan a fishing trip; one year later our family joins a boat club on the St. Croix River. Based on the campaign's success, I assume other dads reacted similarly.

Most people are surprised to find out the ad was sponsored by the boating industry, not the fishing industry. Why did they choose fishing to sell boats? Obviously, in most cases, you need a boat to fish, and with 34.5 million lapsed and occasional anglers in the U.S. who don't currently own a boat, that's an attractive target. But the real beauty of the campaign, its true brilliance, stemmed not from this fact but from a deep insight about human nature.

There's an old saying in boating circles: The two happiest days of boat ownership are the day you buy your boat and the day you sell it. Not surprisingly, the anticipated regret of boat ownership represents a major hurdle for boat manufacturers.

But someone, either on the client or the agency side, knew something about human nature. In the book *Stumbling on Happiness*, Daniel Gilbert explains that we perceive we'll have greater regret for things we *didn't* do, than for things we *did* do.[41] In other words, I envision myself regretting that my daughter leaves the nest before I've had enough special memories with her, more than I would having to sell a boat I rarely use. Buying a boat is reversible; losing time with my daughter is not. When she's gone, she's gone.

The spot beautifully leverages this insight by hitting us dads with the one thing we're most crazy about and most protective of: our daughters. How did they get to this insight? I wasn't there, but generally any good questioning of your customer base gets you to the insight level. It might go something like this:

Step one: Collect a group of like-to-fish-but-don't-own-a-boat dads in room. Step two: Once they tell you that their primary resistance to buying a boat is fear of regret (if they rarely used it), ask them if there is anything else in life they think they'd regret more than buying a boat they seldom use. Step three: Wait ten seconds, and some overworked dad will spout, "Not having spent enough time with my kids," to a roomful of other dads, all nodding in agreement as they check their iPhones.

One additional question leads to a powerful insight that leads to a highly successful—and highly creative—campaign. Even better, this idea-link's life isn't over. I'll bet sometime in your career you'll encounter a situation where you need to overcome regret as a purchase barrier. When you do, this link—**People think they'll regret more the things they didn't do than the things they did (Take Me Fishing)**—will jump out of your head. When it does, e-mail me.

Finding consumer insights everywhere you go

The Take Me Fishing campaign is just one example of a consumer insight–based idea-link; there are many more. You can collect this type of idea-link, not just at work, but everywhere you go and with everyone you meet. Even on your wedding anniversary.

To celebrate our twentieth anniversary, my wife and I visited Wales, a picturesque country in the southwestern part of Great Britain. Along its eastern border with England is the quaint village of Hay-on-Wye, where forty or so bookstores compete for tourists' attention. We went in shop after shop, each looking pretty much the same, all smelling of old books. We would wander around the ground floor, pick up a few books, and then mosey on to the next store.

In the eleventh or twelfth store, I was stopped in my tracks by a message painted above the stairway in Olde English script: 71% of Customers Never Go Upstairs.

Hmmm. Why don't they go upstairs? I wondered. So we sauntered up, curious to find all the wonderful things that only twenty-nine percent of the population has ever seen. To our amazement, nearly ninety-five percent of the store's customers had the same idea. Shoppers packed the upstairs.

For most people, this is where the story ends. Not me. Anniversary or no anniversary, I'm going to find out why the owner did this and why we're packed in like morning riders on a London subway. The proprietor tells me that nobody ever went upstairs so she figured she needed to pique their curiosity. To her amazement, once the slogan went up the stairs, so did every shopper, curious to discover what the others were missing.

So what's the idea-link, the insight we take away from an anniversary in Wales? The lesson is that it helps to have a patient spouse when you're fishing for insights. The idea-link: **One way to create traffic or encourage trial is to pique your customer's curiosity (Hay-on-Wye bookstore).** This idea-link is now yours to use when the situation merits. You can even tell my backstory when you come up with the idea. But beware: When you do, people might call you a name. They might say you're creative.

Science and Technology Idea-Links

When inventor Thomas Edison died in 1931, he left behind more than 3.5 million pages of notebooks and letters. The winding trails of invention within them leave a surprising roadmap for scientists seeking to increase their own creativity. As historians at the Thomas A. Edison Papers at Rutgers University poured over the notes and pictures documenting the 1,093 patents in his name, they discovered that his "powerful ability to reason through analogy,"[42] perhaps more than any other trait, led to his legendary inventiveness. Insights Edison gleaned from a technology in one field inspired development of a second technology in a seemingly unrelated field. For example, current-regulating technology developed for the telegraph formed part of his early work on the electric light bulb.

Perhaps the most surprising example of Edison working by analogy appears on the first page of his preliminary patent on motion pictures. "I am experimenting upon an instrument which does for the eye what the phonograph does for the ear," Edison wrote. He later adds, "The invention consists in photographing continuously a series of pictures . . . in a continuous spiral on a cylinder or plate in the same manner as sound is recorded on the phonograph."[43]

So what does this mean for you? First, let's clarify what an idea-link looks like in the world of technology. You possess technology idea-links when you have an understanding of how a specific system or technology works. For example, if you've studied the technology of the human eye, your idea-links include understanding how the cornea's refractive power bends light or how the retina captures light rays and turns them into light impulses. These idea-links can then transfer to other fields, such as camera design.

This ability to transfer technological insights (or idea-links) from one area to another, as Edison did, can only occur if you understand more than one technology. From there, it's easy to see that improving your odds of creative invention becomes a numbers game. The more technical areas and systems you understand, the more technical idea-links you'll own. The more you own, the greater capacity you have to transfer one to a new area and generate a break-through idea.

Think back to my respirator example from chapter three. Do you recall how "the most creative guy in the division" studied breathing systems in nature that he transferred via analogy to industrial respirators? And how Andy Ouderkirk studied color and lighting systems in nature, which he transferred to your computer screen? Both had moved their understanding beyond the mandatory technologies required for their jobs. They stretched themselves. To become more creative, you must as well.

Second- and third-ring inspiration

If you think about technologies as concentric circles, imagine your core technologies as the inner circle. The first ring from the center contains other technologies used in your industry that you're not required to understand, but likely know anyway. For example, if you're a food scientist, you may not work with retort technology (canning), but you may understand how it works.

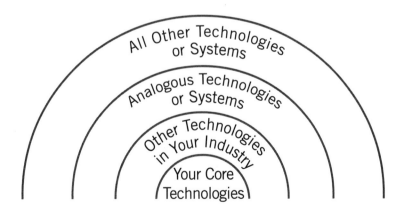

Few explore the second ring—analogous technologies in different industries—including ones found in nature. This second ring is where many breakthrough ideas occur. Ouderkirk transferring butterfly-wing technology to optical film. FedEx founder Fred Smith transferring clearinghouse technology from banks to package delivery. Edison transferring phonograph technology to motion pictures.

Fewer still venture into the third. The third ring contains all the other technologies and systems that appear unrelated to the problems you face and the technologies you use, but still hold potential for breakthrough invention. The movie *Flash of Genius* is a perfect demonstration of the seemingly serendipitous nature of the third ring. In the flash-of-genius scene that inspired the title, the constant back-and-forth motion of windshield wipers irritates the one good eye of engineering professor Robert Kearns. Having lost his other eye to a champagne cork on his honeymoon, Kearns was already keenly aware of how the eye works (one scene shows him studying his eye in his bedroom mirror). While his wipers screech back and forth annoyingly across his windshield, he wonders why his windshield wipers couldn't work more like his eye, which always blinks at the perfect rate. His idea: Windshield wipers that "blink" at optimal rates like eyes do. Today we call Kearns's invention intermittent wipers. And we hail him as a creative genius.

Scientists who have more serendipitous moments than other scientists aren't luckier. They've taken their curiosity beyond the first ring into the second, and then onto the third, filling their brains with idea-links along the way. Since successful transfers from these outer-ring technologies to your problem are only obvious in hindsight, the only way to improve your chances of having one is to dig into as many technologies and systems as you can.

Edison famously said, "Genius is 1% inspiration and 99% perspiration." Now you know where to expend the ninety-nine percent.

New Subject Areas

Sometimes you need to get creative in an altogether new field, perhaps one where you have little or no formal experience. Writing this book is a good example. I am not trained professionally as a writer, but once I decided to write a book and realized no one would do it for me, I deliberately searched for idea-links—or methods for collecting idea-links—in the field of writing.

Someone told me about a poet friend in New Mexico who finds inspiration by paying attention to interesting word combinations. Wherever she goes, whoever she's talking to, if she hears two or more words together that have an appealing ring to them, or a phrasing that sounds pleasing to her ear, she writes it down. These are the idea-links that form the raw material for her creative process. It works for her, so I started to do the same.

I met Will Weaver, an award-winning author from northern Minnesota. (His short story "Gravestone Made of Wheat" inspired the movie *Sweet Land*.[44]) In his stories, Will weaves a vivid tapestry of images like none I've ever read. He describes characters and scenes with such stunning detail that you can't read his books without creating a complete image in your mind at the same time. It's like seeing the movie in your head while you're reading the book.

How does Weaver create such rich detail? "I paid attention to the fragments from my youth," Weaver told me. My youth is gone, but it's not too late to start noticing the intricate detail of the world around me.

I took Michael Snell's advice about finding writing with an "absorbing effect" and then studied how different authors created theirs.[45] In particular, I focused on writers whose style I enjoy. One of my favorites, Peggy Noonan, is a columnist for the *Wall Street Journal*. Noonan's content is always fresh, insightful, and controversial, which is certainly a big part of her appeal, but I wondered why I find her style especially engaging. I noticed Noonan sometimes follows a couple of lengthy sentences, similar to the one I've just written and the one I'm writing now, with a series of short, truncated sentences that technically aren't even sentences, but flow well nonetheless. You'll notice from time to time, I've attempted to do the same in this book. Not everywhere. Just here and there. It works.

The point is, if a hack like me can learn to become a more creative writer in a relatively short time, you can learn to become more creative in your field, regardless of your current level of experience, regardless of your current level of creativity.

What If Your Subject Area Isn't Covered Here?

First, visit the TheNewCreativity.com. There, you'll find a bonus section on Sales Idea-Links. Depending on when you bought the book, you may find more. If I haven't covered areas relevant to your profession here or on the website, share the book with a coworker you think might be similarly motivated. Brainstorm how and where you might find idea-links that will make you more creative in your field. For example, if you're a teacher, study what makes the Khan Academy videos so engaging, or why millions of viewers eagerly tune in to watch Dr. Oz vividly demonstrate how hemorrhoids form or how nipples invert. If you find some good idea-links in a field or area not already mentioned, or want to add idea-links to an existing area, email me or go to the website and click on the Extras tab. I'm continually finding and adding new ones, but I'm more curious to read yours. Now that you've bought the book, we're in this together.

The Old Creativity	The New Creativity
Individuals are responsible for their own creativity.	Individuals can work in teams to build their collective creativity for a subject area.

7

Finding Idea-Links for Specific Projects or Problems

Quiz time. What do the following have in common?

The Navy Seals training program

The best-selling book *Built to Last*

The McDonald's Value Menu

If you know the answer, chances are you're either lucky, or you're a Duck—as in a fan of the hugely successful University of Oregon Ducks football program, guided by football genius Chip Kelly. Coach Kelly, named one of the One Hundred Most Creative People in Business in the June 2011 issue of *Fast Company*, doesn't care much for the "genius" tag. But from my perspective, he's a true creative genius in the idea-link-making sense. That makes him worth studying.

Kelly joined Oregon as offensive coordinator in 2007, later stepping up to head coach in 2009. Under his leadership, the Ducks finished undefeated in 2010, narrowly losing the National Championship to SEC powerhouse Auburn University. That's remarkable. What's more remarkable is how Kelly did it. Kelly built his Ducks for speed, as many college teams do. But Kelly's type of speed is only partly explained by foot speed; his players are no faster than those on other highly ranked teams. What sets the Ducks apart is how fast Kelly gets signals to them from the sidelines and how quickly they line up and run a play. For you diehard football fans, here are just a couple of stats from the 2010 season. Sixteen of Oregon's touchdown drives took less than fifty-six seconds. The Ducks led the nation in points and yards per game, even though they were eighth lowest in the number of minutes per possession.[46]

In one game, they ran plays off about every thirteen seconds; that includes the time it took to run the play itself. In that game, Oregon's final touchdown came on the last of nine consecutive rushing plays. The final play commenced *five seconds* after the completion of the previous play.[47]

For those of you who don't follow football, I'll put Oregon's speed into perspective. The average college team takes about thirty-four seconds from the end of one play to start the next one. Compared to Oregon's thirteen seconds, watching the Ducks between plays is like speeding up your DVD player from "play" to "fast forward," hitting the fast forward button not once but twice. Now imagine what that might look like on your television screen. That's how much faster Oregon gets things done between plays.

Kelly credits Jim Collins, author of bestselling business classics like *Good to Great* and *Built to Last*, with the idea that success in football, as in business, depends on having a clear, easy-to-understand core mission. Kelly says, "If someone says to me, 'What do you stand for?' I should be able to invite them to practice and in five minutes, they'd say: 'I see it. I get it.' They stand for playing hard and playing fast."[48]

If speed is Kelly's strategic focus, his creativity is in how he makes speed happen more efficiently with his team than other coaches do with their teams. The trick was to come up with a communication system for a no-huddle offense that was quick and easy for the Ducks to understand, yet impossible for the opposing team to decipher. Kelly's innovation: Giant signboards with four simple pictures, such as a tiger, a shamrock, or a photo of an ESPN personality. These quick-read images replace the elaborate sequence of hand-signals other teams employ to send in plays.[49]

"It's just another way to play fast," Kelly says. "The analogy I can give you is, if you go to McDonald's and order a No. 2, that's all you have to say and you get a Quarter Pounder and a drink and fries, and you just say, 'No. 2.' If we send them to the board, one picture can mean the formation and the play and the snap-count. That's all it is. It's just another way to play faster."[50]

So far, so good. That accounts for *Built to Last* and the McDonald's Value Menu in the quiz I gave you at the beginning of the chapter. How do the Navy Seals figure in? Kelly says he designed the training for his squad by drawing from documentaries he's seen on military training: "You see how they train the Navy Seals. They squirt them with water, play loud music and do all these other things when they have to perform a task. That's how we practice. We want to bombard our kids."[51]

So what makes Kelly such a brilliant innovator? Why is he considered so creative? It's not really about the Seals, the

Value Menu, or *Built to Last*. To find the good stuff, you need to dig deeper. That means studying what Kelly does to find his ideas, not stealing the ideas themselves.

Kelly draws inspiration from the world around him; not randomly, but with purpose. He deliberately extracts idea-links from areas that are analogous to the goals he wants to achieve or the problems that keep him from reaching those goals. He wanted speed of communication, so he used the McDonald's Value Menu as an idea-link source. A company built on speed of service and, by extension, speed of communication, like McDonald's, is an obvious choice in hindsight, but how many of us would've thought to look there? Shouldn't an industry with the word "fast" in its very descriptor—fast food—deliver some inspiration in your goal to become faster communicators? That's a perfect place to look.

When Kelly realized that a barrier to quick communication was on-field distractions, like crowd noise and defensive players who constantly shift and bark along the line of scrimmage, he dredged from his memory a setting far from the gridiron; a setting where young men are taught the discipline of ignoring the world around them to achieve a mission. He took what worked from Navy Seal training videos and reapplied it to his football program.

Kelly's project or goal was to make his team faster by finding ways to help them communicate better. He did it by identifying the right places to find inspiration. What about your project?

Let Analogies Be Your Guide

We've all been there, staring at our problem, trying to figure out how we're going to crack it. Where will we find the inspiration? When will the ideas come? One thing is certain—if you sit there passively, nothing will happen. In this chapter, I'm going to show you how to make your mind more creative about a particular problem or creative challenge, just as Coach Kelly did.

Like many of you, I'm handed creative problems to solve. But my job is a bit different because about half the time, I'm not the one coming up with the ideas. Instead, I'm figuring out how to help others come up with their own ideas. This is the basic skill behind planning an ideation session—not just thinking, but thinking about how I want others to think. In the process of doing that, my job is less about figuring out *how* you'll find ideas, and more about *where* you'll find them. In that sense, I work like a fishing guide, leading people to the spots most likely to contain the idea-links that will create the best ideas. Not all the spots will work out, but I've got to try them all because I never know for sure where the lunkers lurk. Neither will you.

When it comes to finding the places to become more creative about a specific project or how to creatively reach a specific goal, my go-to divining rod is the analogy. No creative technique is more celebrated or has a longer history than the analogy. Analogies frame the wisdom of Aesop's fables, Christ's parables, Solomon's proverbs, and Buddhist koans. And analogies are behind innovations like the Colt .45 repeating pistol (inspired by the chambers of the ship's wheel), the doctor's stethoscope (inspired by children tapping sounds through a log), and the founding of FedEx (inspired by the bank clearinghouse model).

Analogies continue to inspire us, as demonstrated by the Oregon Ducks and, coincidentally, this book. My breakthrough for understanding and explaining creativity sprang from my comparison of improving one's creativity to organizing one's life, then drawing parallels. Organization was the place I looked.

Most of the famous analogy-inspired inventions have one other aspect in common beyond the means of the inspiration—the discovery itself was accidental. When Dr. René Laënnec invented the stethoscope, he probably wasn't thinking, "I need a better way to have the heart's sound transmitted to my ears, so let's look at other ways sound is transmitted from one location to another."[52] Most of us don't actively think about what our challenge is similar to, and then analyze a series of analogous situations for idea-links. But what if we did? What if we made a habit of actively seeking out analogous situations for the idea-links we need to creatively solve our problems?

> *Most of us don't actively think about what our challenge is similar to, and then analyze analogous situations for idea-links. But what if we did?*

For example, if you work as a new-product marketer on carpet care, what if you instinctively knew to look to shampoos for inspiration because, fundamentally, they are similar? That might lead you to an idea for a product that makes your carpet softer, like conditioner does for your hair. Or a product that removes all the accumulated soap in your carpet fibers, like clarifying shampoos do. Or a product that activates with heat, as Thermasilk does. Or a product that restores the strength of carpet fibers, like the way some shampoos claim to restore damaged or thinning hair. Or a product that . . . you get the idea. And that's from looking at just one outside category. Looking at dental care would conjure up a new host of carpet-care ideas.

When was the last time you used an analogy to solve a problem? "What's this problem similar to?" It's not a question we're trained to ask, or a way we're encouraged to think. Analogies come naturally to some people and are more difficult to grasp for others. Remember those standardized test questions from your youth that asked you to fill in "umbrella is to rain, as *A) fire extinguisher* or *B) cat* is to fire"? Some of you loved those questions; some of you picked "cat." If analogies don't come to you easily, or even if they do, I've developed a simple technique that will help you arrive at more of them.

BreakDown Questions

The key to thinking in analogies is learning how to break your problem down to its most fundamental components, which is why I call this technique the BreakDown Process. Like the other techniques in this book, I purposefully keep it simple so you can more readily make it part of what you'll eventually do out of habit.

Having worked on many hundreds of creative challenges, I've found two basic types: problems where we seek to accomplish or gain something, and problems where we seek to overcome something. Each leads to a different question.

BreakDown Question 1: What do I want to accomplish and who has already accomplished the same thing? Coach Kelly wanted faster communication, so he looked to the fast food industry.

BreakDown Question 2: What are the barriers to solving my problem and who has dealt with similar barriers? Coach Kelly wanted to overcome the distractions that hinder communication. He looked to Navy Seal instructional videos to solve that problem.

For some creative challenges, you can use both questions. But, usually, depending on how you've framed your challenge, one works better than the other. The key discriminating question to ask is whether you're seeking to gain something (question one) or figuring out how to remove or overcome something (question two). Kelly went to McDonald's to gain speed, but went to the Navy Seals to figure out how to remove or overcome distractions. In the end, idea-links from both areas contributed to making his team play faster and communicate better, but each question leads to different sets of analogies. That's why I normally recommend you break down your creative challenge both ways.

Let's do a few examples together for each BreakDown Question. I'll describe each example, but I'll also present it graphically at the end. The resulting visual is another tool for you to use: an Idea-Link Map—a graphic representation of all the places you'll visit to find your idea-links. It can also serve as a collecting point for the idea-links you find and the ideas you generate. The map also shows others how your ideas connect back to an original source of inspiration. These two tools, BreakDown Questions and Idea-Link Maps, are partners in helping you find the idea-links you need and capture them in a way that's user-friendly.

BreakDown Question 1: What do I want to accomplish and who has already accomplished the same thing (with an end result similar to the one I desire)?

Let's pretend we're working for a company that makes protection products for automobiles. They've asked us to generate new product ideas for their core business: The protection and enhancement of interior car surfaces (dashboards, upholstery, steering wheels, and such). Do any ideas jump to mind? Unless you're a serious car buff, recently had a problem with your car interior, or spend a lot of time in back seats, probably not.

Idea-Link Map

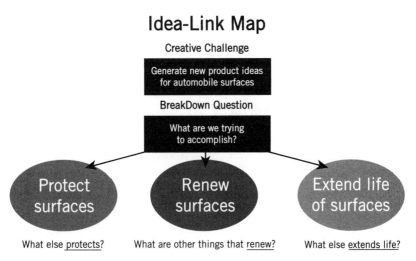

Rather than mulling the question over and over, use the first BreakDown Question: What are we trying to accomplish? The question is sort of a strategic step back. It's time to consider the different outcomes that might be acceptable—not the specific ideas, but what end results we might consider positive. At this point you could list many possible outcomes and pursue them all, or simply pick the ones you like the best. For this example, I'm going to identify three outcomes that might be of value: Protect surfaces (the obvious one), renew surfaces, and extend the life of surfaces.

You could argue that *extending the life of surfaces* is merely a consequence of *protecting surfaces*. Yes, that's correct. But what's important is that they're worded differently, and it's the different wording that can lead you to different examples, which leads to different idea-links, which ultimately leads to different ideas. Different ways of wording the outcome is part of what makes the process work.

For each outcome, think about others who have successfully achieved this in different places or in different ways. At this point you can move far afield from your own category, because sharing the same outcome will maintain some degree of relevance, regardless of how dissimilar the category may be in other ways.

Outcome: Protect surfaces

If we take *protect surfaces*, we ask ourselves who or what else protects surfaces. We also need to think about the term *surfaces* broadly, and not default to thinking about car-type surfaces such as leather or vinyl. Skin is a surface and there are lots of products that have made millions of dollars protecting it. So one of the first places to consider looking for idea-links is skin care. This is where you put on your analytical hard hat and begin systematically disassembling what's working and why. As we search, we're looking for examples of how they've used technology, how they've positioned products, how they've segmented markets, how they've packaged products, how they've sold them, and how they've grown categories

One of the biggest categories in skin care is sun protection. What idea-links could you repurpose from the suntan lotion or sunscreen category? Could you assign a sun protection factor (SPF) to your spray to show it's more effective than other sprays with a lower SPF? How about a disappearing color indicator that gives you confidence you've protected your entire dash from harmful UV rays? Maybe a different kind of indicator that tells you when it stopped blocking UV rays so you know to reapply it? Maybe a spray that once applied actually reflects the sun's rays so your steering wheel won't scald your hands in summer? Even though not all of these ideas come directly from the sunscreen category, digging into it opens up an entire new area of exploration: new ways of defeating the sun.

Outcome: Renew surfaces

Moving on to *renew surfaces*, we can focus specifically on the renewal of surfaces, or look at renewal more broadly. Renewal of surfaces, if we stay in skin care, leads us to wrinkle creams. Renewal in a more general sense might lead us to products that make us feel renewed or young again, such as erectile dysfunction (ED) medicines like Cialis. Let's explore both areas for fruitful analogies.

One of the ways wrinkle creams work is by filling wrinkles. The idea-link is a simple one: **Filling spaces can enhance the appearance of a surface (Olay).** The idea for our car product comes quickly as well—a product that fills the microscopic cracks that materialize in car surfaces over time. By filling these cracks, it prevents dirt, dust, and oils from accumulating, thereby keeping your car surfaces looking new. That was easy.

I bet you're wondering what we can do with ED meds. Cialis was a late arrival to the ED wars, but quickly grabbed a sizeable share away from Viagra.[53] Their point of difference:

After taking Cialis, the medicine stays in the background for forty-eight hours, "activating" only during those moments when the mood strikes (one commercial would suggest that watching your wife wash vegetables is one of those moments). This result is different from Viagra, which holds its effect for a shorter period of time, requiring advanced planning and potentially ruining all those wonderfully spontaneous, vegetable-washing moments that typically lead to sack time.

So here's the idea-link behind Cialis's success: **Create a product that has a longer activation period, but activates only when it's needed (Cialis).** This leads to the idea of creating an interior surface protector that only activates when the sun shines on it. Because it only activates when needed, perhaps we can claim that our "smart" protectant lasts longer than other "dumb" protectants that are depleted over time, regardless of whether the sun is shining on them or not. Is it feasible? Is it a good idea? Who knows, but it's certainly one we wouldn't arrive at by staring into space.

Outcome: Extend the life of surfaces

Our final outcome is *extend the life of surfaces*. What else extends life? How about cholesterol medicines? Statins are a class of wonder drug that extend the lives of millions of Americans and allow us to scarf bacon without fear of reprisal: "I'll have the bacon burger; Lipitor do your thing!" A bit of analysis of the category will reveal another Cialis-like latecomer that grabbed a sizeable share of the market, Vytorin. Vytorin wasn't the first statin, just the first claiming to treat the two sources of cholesterol, food and family history.

Here's our idea-link: **Create a product that treats multiple sources of an ailment or problem; doing so suggests that others**

do not (Vytorin). Now, think about the different sources of interior damage to your car. Do any of the current products treat more than one? If not, can you create a dashboard or upholstery protectant that fights the two sources of premature interior surface aging? If you can, you might be able to mimic Vytorin's success in statins.

Are any of these ideas good ones? At this stage, none of us know whether they'll spark consumer interest or are even feasible. I've made them up as demonstrations. What we do know is that each one is rooted in a success found elsewhere, in an area that's related in principle to our focus area. That improves our chances of success. And we know that without actively searching for idea-links in these areas, we might never have invented the ideas in the first place.

Completing your Idea-Link Map

Our final Idea-Link Map ends up looking something like the figure on the next page.

How many different outcomes and analogies should you look at? That depends on the project and how much time you have. I typically map mine out by hand on a four-by-six-foot sheet of butcher paper, so I can include lots of detail and explore many areas for idea-links. For reasons of brevity, we pursued just a few different outcomes, and then only one analogous example within each outcome. Typically, I would consider more outcomes than just these three, then search for at least ten analogous examples within each outcome, some close-in to my problem and some far-flung.

For example, if you're an aging technology brand and the outcome you choose is "revitalizing my brand" you might look close-in for an example, like Intel's "Intel inside," or move far afield and analyze how Betty White's career "revitalized" at the age of eighty-nine. I refer to less obvious analogies, like the Betty White example, as "novel analogies" because they are more likely to result in novel solutions. But what you gain in newness, you lose in hit rate. Be prepared for some of your novel analogies to lead nowhere. I refer to close-in analogies as "success analogies": more likely to lead you to a usable idea, but less likely to represent anything dramatically different. The best maps cover the entire spectrum, giving you an even blend of both novel and immediately practical ideas.

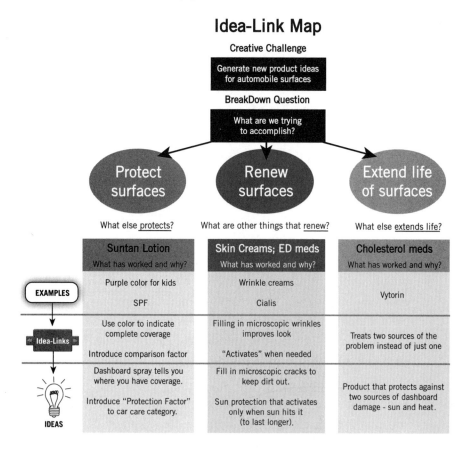

Idea-Link Map

Creative Challenge

Generate new product ideas for automobile surfaces

BreakDown Question

What are we trying to accomplish?

Protect surfaces	Renew surfaces	Extend life of surfaces
What else <u>protects</u>?	What are other things that <u>renew</u>?	What else <u>extends life</u>?
Suntan Lotion	**Skin Creams; ED meds**	**Cholesterol meds**
What has worked and why?	What has worked and why?	What has worked and why?
Purple color for kids	Wrinkle creams	Vytorin
SPF	Cialis	
Use color to indicate complete coverage	Filling in microscopic wrinkles improves look	Treats two sources of the problem instead of just one
Introduce comparison factor	"Activates" when needed	
Dashboard spray tells you where you have coverage.	Fill in microscopic cracks to keep dirt out.	Product that protects against two sources of dashboard damage - sun and heat.
Introduce "Protection Factor" to car care category.	Sun protection that activates only when sun hits it (to last longer).	

EXAMPLES

Idea-Links

IDEAS

Ultimately, you can make your Idea-Link Map as big or as involved as you want, doing it alone or as a team of twenty. What matters is the common structure. By following it, you'll all be on the same page, literally, using the same process and language.

Another way to build an Idea-Link Map and break down a creative challenge is to dissect why it's a challenge in the first place. Rarely does a problem originate from one source; usually it has multiple culprits and contributors. When you break down the problem into its individual culprits, you can then explore how others have attacked a similar aspect of the problem and steal their idea-links. It doesn't matter if the "others" are similar to you or not; again, you'll get more unique ideas the further afield you look. Which brings us to our next example, BreakDown Question two.

BreakDown Question 2: What are the barriers to solving my problem and who has dealt with similar barriers?

Let's say you're the director of sales for a phone retailer such as Verizon or Sprint. You've noticed your retail sales-people stay busy, but have difficulty closing the sale. Since we suspect this is more a problem of overcoming barriers, we ask the second BreakDown Question: What are the barriers to my problem? We ask around various locations and discover many reasons for the poor close rate, but for brevity we'll focus on just three:

Product knowledge: Too many products to sift through

Lackluster incentives: Too boring to get salesperson's attention

Time pressure: Need to get to the next customer quickly

Product knowledge: Too many products to sift through

The sheer number of options is overwhelming to customers and sales staff alike. So we ask ourselves who excels at streamlining information, or providing shortcuts to large amounts of product or content? How about television networks? TV shows condense lots of information into thirty- or sixty-minute windows. What have they done that works? What about the Travel Channel, which takes millions of possible destinations, categorizes them by type (romantic getaways, waterparks, etc.), then presents them in a Top Ten List format. Could we create a Top Three List for each customer type based upon popularity? Top three phones for moms. Top three for dads. Top three for under twelve. Top three for college. Top three for music lovers. You get the idea. By instantly narrowing the search to three, customers reach decisions faster and more walk out with cell phones in their bags. It's a win-win-win for the customer, salesperson, and company.

Creating a Top Three List by customer type is a solution that's obvious only in hindsight. The Travel Channel seems a million miles away from a retail cellular outlet until you realize they share the same challenge. Focusing less on your problem and more on the *elements* of your problem, such as barriers and challenges, will routinely lead you to see obvious-in-hindsight solutions that might remain undiscovered with your old way of thinking.

Lackluster incentives: Too boring to gain attention

Making your incentives less boring leads you to ask, how have others created excitement? Or what causes excitement?

The list is endless, but lotteries jump to my mind. One of the more exciting lottery features is the Powerball, a random item that multiplies your winnings. What if we added a Powerball element to our incentives? Could you imagine if once a month, on some totally random day, the sales incentive rose by a factor of four? Or ten? The combination of the randomness and the multiplier makes your incentive much more exciting and memorable. And where there's excitement, motivation is not far behind.

Time pressure: Need to get to the next customer quickly

If your sales force feels time pressure to move from one customer to another before they've closed the sale, ask yourself who else deals with similar time pressure. What about emergency-room nurses? Can you apply the concept of triage to your sales floor? Is there a way to quickly segregate customers by type, such as existing customers and new customers? Perhaps your commissioned employees only deal with new customers, and your noncommissioned sales force works with existing customers. That also allows you to put your most accomplished sellers on your new prospects (spending as much time as needed) and your best problem solvers on your existing customers (solving their problems quickly). Everyone's happy and sales jump.

I've given you a quick glance at the second BreakDown Question, with a limited number of examples so you'll understand it without getting bored. In real life, if a problem like this is important to your team, you'll spend much more time exploring many more analogous situations. Our beginning map looks something like this:

Idea-Link Map

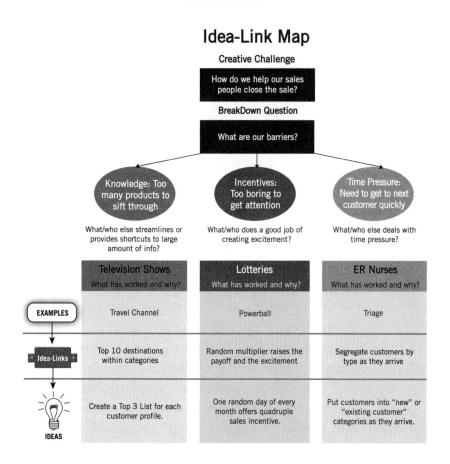

Creative Challenge

How do we help our sales people close the sale?

BreakDown Question

What are our barriers?

Knowledge: Too many products to sift through	Incentives: Too boring to get attention	Time Pressure: Need to get to next customer quickly
What/who else streamlines or provides shortcuts to large amount of info?	What/who does a good job of creating excitement?	What/who else deals with time pressure?
Television Shows What has worked and why?	**Lotteries** What has worked and why?	**ER Nurses** What has worked and why?
EXAMPLES — Travel Channel	Powerball	Triage
Idea-Links — Top 10 destinations within categories	Random multiplier raises the payoff and the excitement	Segregate customers by type as they arrive
IDEAS — Create a Top 3 List for each customer profile.	One random day of every month offers quadruple sales incentive.	Put customers into "new" or "existing customer" categories as they arrive.

Looking to the Outside

Both BreakDown Questions, and analogies in general, have one thing in common: They compel you to look not only inside, but also *outside* your company, category, or functional area to find new idea-links to help you solve your creative challenges. Since they're outside your company or industry but still related to your problem in principle, these kinds of idea-links are a powerful source of new ideas to help you solve your problem.

Looking to the outside is nothing new, but most companies do it the wrong way. Benchmarking other categories and companies is one thing, but it won't lead you to new ideas—it won't make you more creative. But when you look to the outside with the intent of extracting idea-links, you build your company's idea-generating potential and improve your chances of solving tough creative challenges. Remember, when it comes to creativity, the one with the most idea-links wins, and looking outside is a great place to find them.

Also, don't let the deliberate nature of the idea-link hunting we've done in this and the last chapter prevent you from continuing to notice the idea-link-making opportunities that come to you by chance. You get new idea-links two ways: first, by purposely seeking idea-links related to your job or your project, and second, by pouncing on idea-link-making moments as they come, whether or not they seem relevant at the time. Idea-links from both sources hold the potential to solve your problem.

Saving and Sharing Your Creative Assets

In chapter five we covered how to record and store idea-links. Now that you're ready to start gathering them for your job or your project, I need to stress again the importance of writing them down. Think of your idea-links as valuable creative assets, each capable of generating an idea now or in the future. We protect other kinds of corporate assets we've worked hard to develop—our trademarks, our people, our

We protect other kinds of corporate assets we've worked hard to develop— so why should we treat idea-links any differently?

processes, our secret recipes—so why should we treat idea-links any differently? You've worked hard to extract these idea-links, so spend just a bit more time and find a way to preserve them.

Getting idea-links written down somewhere, somehow, serves two purposes. First, you can share them across your current team—keeping them in your head only advances your creativity, not the collective creativity of your team or company. Thinking of creativity as the mysterious gift of the isolated few is the old way of thinking. The new way is to think of idea-links as shared assets, where adding more idea-links to the collective pool raises the creative tide for all boats. Second, recording your idea-links preserves the company's creative assets beyond your time with a department or team and into the future. What matters isn't how recent the idea-link is, but rather how rich and varied the assortment. Understanding the direct relationship between idea-links and creativity turns it into a numbers game. And the only way to accumulate idea-links is to save them.

So when you come up with an idea-link, even if it's just for a specific project, write it down and have it cataloged. It might be your best shot at immortality!

The Old Creativity	The New Creativity
Analogies are an important part of creativity.	Analogies can be systematically and deliberately discovered using BreakDown Questions.

Part Two

Creative

Reframing

Discipline 2

Creative Reframing

So far you've been learning how to stuff more idea-links into your brain to make yourself more creative. Or, if you're thinking about the process from a group perspective, you've seen how to fill your company's creative coffers with idea-links to make your organization or team more creative. While adding idea-links is the single best way to build creativity, there's one more trick, one more discipline you need to learn. That's getting at more of the idea-links you've already stored in your brain and putting them to work to creatively solve your problem.

Each of you started this journey with a brain full of idea-links, swimming around, just waiting to connect to the right problem. Every person, every brain, possesses these links—you can't go through life without having recognized, to some extent, what makes the world around you tick, particularly in the subjects or hobbies that interest you most. Everyone is curious about something. Whatever your interests, you've got idea-links in your brain related to them. You simply didn't know the idea-links were there, because they weren't named or defined . . . until now.

When you go to work in the morning, you'll see your coworkers and guess what? They've got brains full of idea-links, too—even the bleary-eyed hungover guy in the cube down the hall. Some links are similar to yours, but many are entirely different because over the course of our lives, what each person experiences and analyzes varies according to our individual interests.

What if there was a systematic way to get the existing idea-links out of our brains and make them squirm all over the whiteboard, mixing and combining into truly terrific ideas? That's what discipline two of *Idea-Links* is all about.

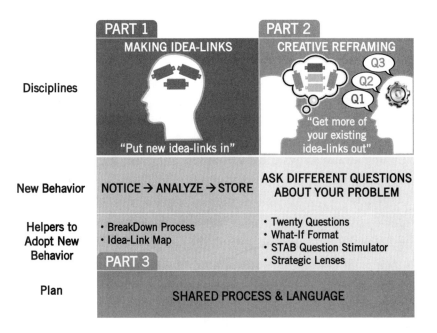

8

Creative Reframing: Accessing Idea-Links You Already Own

To raise new questions, new possibilities, to regard old problems from a new angle, requires creative imagination, and marks real advance in science.

—ALBERT EINSTEIN, SCIENTIST

The greatest challenge to any thinker is stating the problem in a way that will allow a solution.

—BERTRAND RUSSELL, BRITISH AUTHOR AND PHILOSOPHER

When we change the way we look at things, the things we look at change.

—WAYNE DYER, SELF-HELP AUTHOR

What if you got a call tomorrow with the bad news that a family member or close friend needed a kidney? Think for a second—would you at least consider donating one of yours? If you're nodding your head, you're like most people. The prospect of losing a loved one seems more emotionally painful than the physical pain of having your kidney removed. So most of us would, at a minimum, consider offering up a kidney.

What would happen if the test came back and you discovered you weren't an adequate match? How many of you would think, "Since I already blocked out the day on Outlook, why don't I go ahead, get mine cut out, and see if someone else can use it?" Not me, and probably not you either. We're not evil people; it's just that the whole risk/reward ratio suddenly changed. The pain and the risk of donating a kidney to a complete stranger, to whom you have no emotional ties, no longer seems worth it.

Until recently, the main question facing the organizations trying to put a dent in the backlog of 125,000 patients needing kidneys was: "How can we persuade more people to donate both kidneys when they die?" Thanks to numerous public campaigns, more and more people willingly check the little box on their driver's license renewal form that allows organ harvesting upon death or when death is imminent. Yet, despite the success of at- or near-death harvesting, the backlog of people needing kidneys remains daunting.

So we know "How do we get people to donate both kidneys when they die?" is a correct question but ultimately, it fails to adequately deal with the entire backlog problem. If we continue to stare at that same question, we'll continue to come up with the same ideas.

A different creative challenge is overcoming the matching issue. Most everyone is willing to donate . . . to someone they love . . . if they have a match. We just proved that. So let's ask a different question: *What if we solved the matching issue?*

This question looks at the problem from another perspective, which will reveal different solutions. Those of you who think in analogies might naturally begin to ask what other organizations or individuals deal with "matching" problems, particularly where one party is asking another party to give something up, but can't offer an adequate match in return. How do they handle it?

If you're into sports, this follow-up question may prompt you to think about how the National Basketball Association (NBA) trades players. Let's say San Antonio wants Minnesota's point guard, but can only offer a center in return, which Minnesota doesn't need. But a third team, New York, needs San Antonio's center, and happens to have an extra power forward, which Minnesota could use. A deal is struck and each team gets a player who matches their needs. In basketball lingo it's known as a three-team swap; they've been doing it for sixty years because basketball, unlike most sports, involves five—and only five—distinct, specialized positions. When it comes to making trades that benefit both teams, matching is often an issue in the NBA. In those cases, they include a third team and everyone goes home happy.

It wasn't until 2006 that the kidney donation industry took a page from the NBA playbook and arranged its own three-way trade process. The spouse of patient A matches patient B, friend of B matches patient C, and spouse of C matches patient A. This simple idea—the three-way kidney swap—took off and began reducing the waiting list on the kidney registry. But it came with one complication. To prevent one of the parties from backing out after receiving their kidney, all three kidney transplants had to occur simultaneously. That meant only large hospitals could conduct the procedure.

Let's ask yet a different question and see if a different idea emerges: *What if one person—who's willing to give, but isn't a match—gives anyway, with no expectation of anything in return? What would happen next?*

For a few readers, an idea-link will immediately spring forth. For others, it may not until I offer a clue: Think of a movie where someone does something extraordinary for a complete stranger, with the expectation of nothing in return. Now at least ten percent of you have landed on the movie *Pay It Forward. Pay It Forward* is both a movie, and if you recall the principle behind the movie, an idea-link: **One selfless good deed spawns a whole series of good deeds, performed in succession (Pay It Forward).** Pay-it-forward is essentially a business model for encouraging good deeds.

The idea of the pay-it-forward model of kidney donation didn't emerge until 2007. Also known as the "daisy chain" system for its similarities to daisy chains in electrical wiring, this type of kidney donation can be performed sequentially and in different locations across the country. It's predicated on having one selfless individual start the chain by donating to a complete stranger, for no other reason than to do something amazing. From there, a friend of the first recipient "pays forward" her kidney to another complete stranger, and the chain continues. So, when you raise your hand for your brother Bill, he'll get a kidney, but only because you're giving yours to Juan in Mexico City.

The Evolution of Paired Exchange

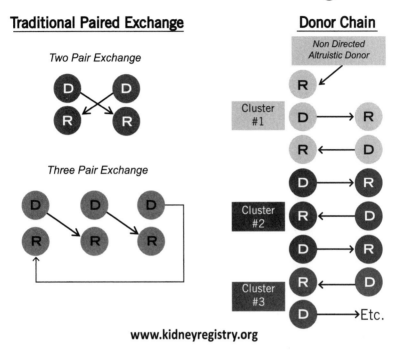

www.kidneyregistry.org

In hindsight, both the three-person kidney swap and the pay-it-forward model of kidney donation are so simple a child could think of them. So how did we miss such obvious ideas all these years? That's the value of asking lots of different questions; that's the power of creative reframing.

Why Creative Reframing Works

Creative reframing is another way to help you solve your problem creatively. If you think of making idea-links as the process of putting more creative raw material *in* your brain, think of creative reframing as the way to get it *out* of your brain. Creative reframing is the process of restating your problem in multiple ways (or asking different questions related to your problem) to bring into view different idea-links or ideas.

Creative Reframing:

Restating your problem in multiple ways or asking different questions to bring into view different idea-links or ideas.

Creative reframing works like magic glasses that help you and others see new connections. Each creative reframing changes your view of the problem. And each new view of the problem has the potential to unlock a unique idea-link, or set of idea-links, or some other connection, from your memory. The more glasses you look through, the more idea-links you'll see. The more idea-links you see, the better your odds of connecting one to your problem.

During the kidney story, I slapped two pairs of glasses on you that allowed us to see new ways to solve the backlog. I'm guessing few of you "saw" the idea-link of how basketball trades work—that was an obscure idea-link that required a specialized knowledge of basketball. Probably more of you saw the pay-it-forward idea-link. If you didn't see either, that's okay. That's why you ask lots of questions, not just a couple. You aren't trying to find the perfect question that leads everyone to see the same answer; you're simply trying to find *a* question where someone sees *an* answer. We asked two different questions and got two different answers or approaches, both of which are different from previous strategies.

Creative reframing not only works, but it's also easy to do—once you get in the habit. Just as making idea-links, the first discipline, requires you to think more deeply about what you encounter, creative framing simply asks you to generate additional questions about your problem. It may require just one new question, or you may need to pose twenty questions until you get to the idea you need.

The term *reframing* isn't new. It originates in family systems therapy, where, for example, a therapist teaches you to think about your meddling mother-in-law not as an annoying meddler but as a valuable family member who provides an unusually high level of protection for your kids. In the context of family systems therapy, reframing is all about changing perspectives so you can begin to see your family interactions and family members differently.

In the context of creativity, reframing is all about changing perspectives so you begin to see your problem differently. Hence the term, *creative reframing*. With each new question, your mind "moves the frame" to a new place in your brain. In these new places, your mind sees new idea-links, whereas when you ask just one question, most of your existing links remain hidden outside the established frame.

The pay-it-forward idea-link was already in your brain. When I asked a different question, your frame shifted and suddenly you saw it. Once you saw it, you could then connect it to your problem in the form of a new idea. Simply stated, you can't connect the dots if you keep looking at the same limited field of dots. Creative reframing reveals different dots.

Recreating the Shower Experience without Getting Wet

Could the concept of creative reframing explain why so many people have ideas in the shower? Here's my theory: While generally pleasurable, the daily shower is probably the most mundane, repetitive activity in most people's lives. Each day, you go to the same place at the same time and do the same thing.

Even the most boring commute still involves some change in scenery: new seasons, new people on the subway, the occasional dead squirrel. Yet the shower scenery stays the same, unless you're rapidly gaining or losing weight, or recently had sex-change surgery. And, unlike driving, there is almost no need to concentrate and no opportunity to do anything else useful. You can't read. You can't text. You can't do Sudoku. Out of this mundane scenario, in this environment of no distractions, the brain is free to mull. Rapid-fire creative reframing occurs like nowhere'else as we cycle through questions: What if this? What if that? Idea-links and ideas come into view. Eureka moments occur.

Next time you come up with an idea in the shower, quickly think back to what triggered the idea. Chances are you asked a question like "I wonder if . . . ," or "I wonder why . . . ," or even "What if we . . . ?" You're either wondering or worrying. And wonderers and worriers are typically very creative people—both are naturally predisposed to create lots of different scenarios in their heads. Different scenarios are nothing more than seeing the problem from different vantage points. Once you understand the shower experience is really just about rapidly and indiscriminately asking lots of questions, with a little work you can re-create the shower eureka magic, without getting wet.

Einstein re-created the same experience, but in a different way. One of Einstein's favorite methods for generating ideas was to gather a group of respected colleagues and ask them to debate a problem from a variety of angles. Dubbed "The Olympia Academy," these esteemed colleagues posed questions deep into the night. It wasn't the group's ideas Einstein sought, but rather the questions they raised—different questions from the ones he was asking. The secret to unearthing idea-links that already exist in your brain (and the brains of your coworkers and friends) is asking more questions about whatever you're working on. But if it's that simple, and obvious, why aren't we asking more questions now?

Being Creative Versus Being Right

Being *right* and being *creative* are not the same thing. We spend most of our adult lives seeking to ask the right question—the one perfect question that succinctly captures the issue at hand or nails precisely the problem we're trying to solve. Much of our professional training reinforces this notion, whether we're getting an MBA, law degree, or engineering degree. We learn to identify and define the key issue or problem, spending considerable time getting the wording just right. And that's a good thing. Without agreement on the key issues, there's no alignment among team members, no sense of direction. We get rewarded on performance reviews for asking the right questions, and rightfully so.

Yet, when it comes to generating creative solutions, remaining fixated on a single right question is a bad thing. Without the new vantage points offered by multiple questions, you're unable to see new paths, even when they're right behind, beside, or in some cases, right in front of you. The same question again and again—even though it's the *right* one—gets you the same set of idea-links and the same list of tired solutions. It's for this reason that breakthrough ideas often come from industry outsiders or from new entrants to a market. They don't know the right questions, they just ask questions. And sometimes their questions lead to startling new realizations that hadn't occurred to the insiders who are practiced at finding the *right* questions.

> *When it comes to finding new and novel solutions, it isn't about asking the right question. It's all about asking different questions. Lots of them.*

When it comes to finding new and novel solutions, it isn't about asking the right question. It's all about asking different questions. Lots of them. To people who pride themselves in finding the one right question, this can seem outright strange—even wrong. If that sounds like you, you need to reread this paragraph, and then get over it. You're reading this book to become *more creative*, not to become *more right*. Your focus on always asking the right question, to the exclusion of posing new ones, is limiting your creativity.

The medical industry was asking how they could increase the number of people who'd voluntarily donate their kidneys upon death. That wasn't the wrong question, but it was just one question. It was worthwhile to focus on it, but not to the exclusion of all other possible questions.

When we asked other questions, that first question didn't disappear. We just shifted our focus to new questions to see what ideas we'd find.

Creative Reframing in Action

Let's say I asked you to come up with ideas to make shareholder meetings more entertaining or engaging. You should be able to come up with ideas even if it's unrelated to your job experience or you've never attended a shareholder meeting. We can all at least imagine what most shareholder meetings go like: the CEO reports on financials and future prospects, shareholders ask questions, employees give away free trinkets, the date of next year's meeting is announced, parking tickets are validated on the way out. Repeat in 365 days. How can we make it more entertaining or engaging? Take sixty seconds to think of ideas.

Okay, time's up. Maybe you started off with some ideas that came quickly, then petered out at the end of the minute. Maybe you came up with a few ideas, but took a while to get started. Maybe you never even got going—the way the question was worded simply didn't allow you to *see* any ideas. Or you figured since you paid for the book, you'll let me do the work. Fair enough. Regardless of how it worked for you, the point is: Any individual question is limited in the number of ideas it will reveal. Eventually, you'll run out of juice.

Now let's creatively reframe by changing just one element. Instead of the CEO running our meeting—*what if Jay Leno ran our shareholder meeting?* Again, take sixty seconds to think of ideas for making a shareholder meeting more engaging.

Did you see something entirely different? Did you imagine the CEO mixing with the audience before the meeting? Did you imagine clips of "Jaywalking" interviews, asking people what they thought of your products or your competitor's products? Did you imagine a collection of amusing headlines gathered from throughout the year poking fun at the company? (Did you imagine your CEO naming a successor, then changing his mind?)

All these idea-links (the things that work) from Jay Leno's original long-running shtick on *The Tonight Show* reveal themselves within the frame of a new, provocative question. They play a big part in Leno's success, and if reapplied to your problem, could potentially do the same for your shareholder meeting. These Leno idea-links were already camped out somewhere in your brain, ready to connect to your problem. But you only bring them into view and capture them for your current purpose by disciplining yourself to willfully step away from the right question and ask another instead.

In fact, just asking the Leno question opens up an entire strategic area to explore. What can we learn (and steal) from other TV-show formats? Television shows are in the entertainment business, so that's a good analogy to dig into. If we did, we would have pages of new ideas.

Just for fun, let's try one more creative reframing by challenging the assumption that shareholder meetings are inherently boring. *What if we could get people to actually look forward to shareholder meetings?* Think about that for sixty seconds. If you're still struggling, ask a follow-up question: *What types of things do people look forward to in their lives?*

This particular reframing leads me to lots of ideas. People anticipate meeting and seeing people who share common interests and concerns. What about giving shareholders the chance to make new friends with other shareholders based on some kind of commonality? This could be as straightforward as a pre-meeting where people with similar investment concerns gather and ask questions, or as far-fetched as a mixer for widowed or divorced retirees to connect with other single retirees. Before you laugh, remember that retirees make up the bulk of most annual-meeting audiences because the rest of us have to work. And they may be more motivated by a boost in their social life than a boost in their dividend.

People also look forward to annual traditions. Can you think of some to add to a shareholder meeting? As you think about the problem in this way, you begin to uncover what makes Berkshire Hathaway's annual meetings the biggest shareholder party in the history of capitalism. Warren Buffett, one of the richest men on the planet, is also one hell of a party planner. Seemingly hokey events, like the bridge tournament and softball game, are now annual traditions that give shareholders the chance to have fun and meet other shareholders. Compare those settings to the stuffy auditoriums that turn most meetings into a mass coma, and it's easy to see why shareholders look forward to Berkshire Hathaway's annual meetings.

You may not have the budget to create an event on this scale, but I'm guessing if you simply took the time to consider what people look forward to in life, you'll see a whole set of viable ideas that wouldn't have occurred to you by asking only the original question.

So which of these questions was the *right* question: the Leno question, the "look forward to" question, or the original question? If each generated different, but viable ideas, each is right in the creative sense. It's smart to focus on the right *objective*, but labeling one question the right question implies that all other questions are wrong questions. In the process, we mentally discard all questions but the right one and unwittingly leave a raft of different and potentially better ideas undiscovered.

The Twenty Questions Exercise

How do you transform yourself from a right-question person to a many-questions person? It involves that pesky word again: discipline.

Remember the game Twenty Questions? One person thinks of the answer, usually something like an animal, famous person, or household object, then the other person asks questions to gradually limit the field to one possible answer. If the answer is revealed in fewer than twenty questions, the questioner wins.

To get yourself into the discipline of asking multiple questions, you need to adopt your own Twenty Questions game. Each time you have a creative challenge, make it a game to generate twenty new questions about your problem. At first, it will feel like work. It takes effort to stop what you're doing, sit down, and consciously crank out more questions than you might usually ask. But thinking of it as a game, or as a challenge to yourself, will make it feel easier.

To practice, I'll pick as the subject area something we all do: take showers. Pretend you're the research and development manager for a company that makes showers (such as show-erheads and showering systems). Your job is to continually create a stream of shower innovations. Write down: *In what ways can we make showers or showering better or different?* That's our objective. That's our *right* question.

If you have paper handy, start writing questions, numbering each one (doing it in your head won't work). For the purpose of simplicity, start all your questions with "what if." I'll explain why that's important in the next chapter.

Give yourself about five minutes to generate twenty what-if questions, stopping either when you hit the five-minute mark, or when you get to twenty questions, whichever comes first. There will be moments when your brain comes to a halt—don't panic. Work through it, keep mulling, and the questions will come. If you're finding it extremely diffi-cult and never get to twenty, don't get discouraged. In the next chapter, I'll give you a tool that will make it much easier. But for now, I want you to try it on your own.

Once you have twenty questions or five minutes have passed, consider each question for about thirty seconds, letting the question take your brain where it will. Some will trigger ideas. Some will trigger new questions. As ideas surface, write them down or make mental note of them.

My list of questions is in the box below. After you've gone through your questions, read mine over, one by one, and see if any new ideas emerge as you ponder each one.

In what ways can we make showers or showering better or different?

1. What if showers could talk?

2. What if showers were like baths?

3. What if a shower knew how much money I had?

4. What if showers were the best part of my day?

5. What if every shower I took was different?

6. What if the shower had a time limit?

7. What if taking a shower was like driving a car?

8. What if showers didn't have to warm up?

9. What if showers could clean themselves?

10. What if showers were upside down?

11. What if showers didn't wake us up?

12. What if more than water came through the shower head?

13. What if there was no shower head?

14. What if a shower didn't use water?

15. What if my dog could take a shower?

16. What if kids designed their own shower?

17. What if showers made your bathroom less expensive?

18. What if we combined a shower with another appliance?

19. What if a shower did more than just make me clean?

20. What if a shower gave me ideas?

After reading my list of questions, you probably generated different ideas than you did with your own questions. That's how creative reframing works. The more people you have asking questions, the more questions you get. The more questions you consider, the more ideas you'll generate. Once you know this formula, it's a simple numbers game.

When you looked through the questions, you probably noticed that what-if questions work in many different ways to trigger ideas.

> A question may allow you to see a new idea-link that leads directly to an idea, leaving a clear trail (question to idea-link to idea).

> A question may trigger an immediate idea that's untraceable back to an idea-link.

> A question may **be the idea**, such as, "What if we decided to do nothing?" Questions and ideas sometimes arise simultaneously; there is no way to stop that from happening, nor should you try.

> A question may spur other questions, one of which may lead to a new idea. My first question "What if showers could talk?" led me to a follow-up question: "If my shower could talk, what would I want it to tell me?" I might want it to tell me when my shower hits the five-dollar mark in water usage, or I might want it to give me a ten-minute Spanish lesson, or issue my kids a two-minute warning before it shuts itself off. Let one question birth other questions.

I can't fully explain all the reasons and ways that new questions lead to new ideas. They just do. The work part of creativity is thinking of the questions in the first place. Letting the questions take you wherever they lead is the fun and magic part of creativity. It will make the work part seem worth it, so relax and enjoy. You earned it!

You may also have caught yourself judging your questions as you were formulating them. For this exercise to work, you can't get hung up on evaluating your questions for rightness or wrongness, or goodness or badness. What matters isn't how right an idea is in the beginning, but *how revealing each question is in the end.*

For example, my question "What if showers didn't use water?" seems absurd. At first blush, it's a wrong or stupid question. But it made me think about waterless car washes, which already exist, and the broader category of car washes. That made me think of the stages in a car wash, which made me think of the drying cycle at the end. That led me to the idea of a warm-air feature that would dry you off at the end of your shower. So this particular what-if question, while obviously not *right* in the beginning, sent me down a path that's *revealing* in the end.

The thing about revealing questions is you won't know how revealing one is until you write each question down and actually take the time to see what ideas it exposes. Even then, a question that reveals little or nothing for you may unlock the mother of all ideas for your coworker. You'll never know unless you ask it in the first place. No question ventured, no idea gained.

Make Twenty Questions a New Habit

Think about the Twenty Questions exercise as a way to start a new habit—a good habit. It pushes you to overcome your natural inclination to stop at one question, and then beat that poor, lonely question to death. Each time you practice, it transforms your mind from focusing on one right question, to entertaining lots of different questions. Or from a mind that frequently gets stuck, to a mind that explores possibilities, both for yourself and those around you. Eventually, with enough repetition, asking more questions will rub off on your regular thought process. When it does, you will become more creative.

• • •

Any question that comes to you is a potentially fruitful one—but there are also certain types of questions that are especially productive. In the next chapter, I'll give you and your organization a common questioning style and a question-stimulating tool that will help you create twenty questions in a snap.

The Old Creativity	The New Creativity
Everyone should focus on one question because it's the right question.	Everyone should ask lots of questions because they'll reveal more ideas.

What If:
Creativity's Most Potent Question

Imagination is the beginning of creation. You imagine what you desire, you will what you imagine, and at last you create what you will.

—GEORGE BERNARD SHAW, IRISH PLAYWRIGHT

To live a creative life, we must lose our fear of being wrong.

—JOSEPH CHILTON PEARCE, CHILD DEVELOPMENT THEORIST

If you want to make the process of generating questions easier, you'll need to adopt two simple guidelines. First, begin your questions with "What if . . ." While this may seem restrictive at first—or cause you to wonder whether it will actually make the task tougher, not easier—keep an open mind as you read. You'll soon learn that asking what-if questions is anything but restrictive; in fact, it's freeing. Second, commit to memory the STAB question stimulator I'll share with you later in the chapter. The STAB stimulator makes question generation quick, painless, and productive.

First, why the big focus on what-if questions?

We've all heard Einstein's credo, "Imagination is more important than knowledge," but what does that really mean? What about that quote seems so intuitively correct that you find yourself nodding your head in agreement? Perhaps Einstein's greatest creative talent was his ability to conduct thought experiments—the ability to visually *imagine* a what-if scenario in his mind and then *see* the implications it created as the scenario unfolded. They were called *thought* experiments because they didn't occur in a laboratory; they played out entirely in Einstein's imagination. Whether imagining his body pursuing a beam of light or traveling through space in an elevator, Einstein's imaginary what-if scenarios transported his mind to new places, allowing him to see the clues toward new theories that would later revolutionize science.

Ever wonder how bestselling author Stephen King has come up with so many different and bizarre story ideas? On his website King writes, "I get my ideas from everywhere. But, in a lot of cases it's seeing two things and having them come together in some new and interesting way, and then adding the question 'What if?' 'What if' is always the key question."[54]

You may never need to discover the origins of the universe or write a bestselling book, but if this kind of regular, dedicated (and, yes, disciplined) what-if postulating works for them, you can bet it will work for you. Bottom line: Asking what-if questions is a powerful creative habit that can uncover startling new ideas whatever your ultimate goal. Here's what makes the what-if structure so powerful.

Conquering the Dumb Question

We've all heard the saying "There's no such thing as a dumb question." Now let's be truthful. Who among us hasn't been in a meeting or a party, heard someone ask a question, and thought, "Wow, that was one incredibly dumb question!" Like it or not, those experiences stoke our fear of asking our own dumb or seemingly unrealistic questions. We know how we judged the person asking the dumb question, and we don't want others heaping those same scornful thoughts upon us. Unconsciously, we think dumb question equals dumb person, or "dumb is as dumb asks." Fear of sounding dumb may only be a primitive survival instinct gone haywire, but regardless of its origin, apprehension about sounding stupid in front of others prevents many of us from asking as many provocative questions as we could (and should).

One of the reasons what-if questions work is that they remove some of the fear of asking a stupid question and appearing dumb. Why? They're worded in a way that gives the questioner permission to be wrong, or at least impractical. When we start a question with "what if," it serves as cultural shorthand for "here comes a question that might be just a little bit crazy, but could help us see things differently." "What if" says to the audience that the person asking the question *realizes* this possibility isn't likely or realistic, but for the sake of spurring imagination, let's all consider it anyway.

When I asked, "What if Jay Leno ran our shareholder meeting?" it's clear that I wasn't suggesting that Jay Leno should actually pinch hit for your CEO. I'm just inviting you to consider the notion and see what ideas pop up when you do.

Suspending Reality is Not Ignoring Reality

The other powerful aspect of what-if reframing is the freedom it affords. The words *what if* temporarily free you from reality. Once you lose the restrictions of reality, you're free to take your question in hundreds of different directions and see your problem from as many different angles. This means if you consider yourself a realist, you need to see the critical distinction between accepting reality and suspending it. Accepting reality is acknowledging that a situation is real, as are all its related limitations and barriers. Suspending reality allows you to accept what's realistic, but at the same time recognize that—at least during the idea-generation stage—asking only realistic questions can prevent you, and others, from discovering ideas that may lead to your solution.

You may have heard William Gordon's quote, "The ultimate solutions to problems are rational; the process of finding them is not." As Gordon suggests, if you want to generate great ideas, you'll sometimes need to temporarily suspend reality when it comes to which questions you ask. Highly creative people do this all the time, and it's part of the reason they often get the "unrealistic" tag unfairly pinned on them. Creative people aren't unrealistic or igno-rant of reality—they've just learned to temporarily suspend their realistic view of the world to ask themselves and others idea-provoking questions.

Here's another way to think about it. Highly creative people aren't unrealistic because they are creative. Rather, they are creative because they sometimes allow themselves to think unrealistically. It's a skill to think this way, to imagine impossible scenarios like, "What if Jay Leno ran our shareholder meetings?" It takes work and discipline to overcome your natural inclination to think realistically all the time.

I'm not telling you that *all* your questions must be unre-alistic, or that a certain percentage of your questions should be unrealistic and the rest realistic. Nor should you now begin grading your questions for how unrealistic they are. If you do that, you've created the same judging problem, only reversed.

Remember earlier in the book I told you the first two adjectives I would use to describe creative people—inquisitive and acquisitive? The third might surprise you: unrestricted. What I mean by *unrestricted* is that they're able to question without constraints. It doesn't mean they're undisciplined or unrealistic as people. Unrestricted thinking is the ability to imagine possibilities or scenarios that may not be true, or are clearly impossible, purely for the sake of seeing where it leads you.

Others have called this ability *playfulness*, which is a poor and misleading descriptor. Playfulness is not viewed as a thinking trait as much as it is a personality trait. Plenty of people have the ability to think about a problem in many different ways, but you wouldn't describe their personalities as playful. While this may sound like a lecture in semantics, labels matter. If a group of people came to me seeking advice on how to become more creative, and I told them they needed to act more playful, many would turn away and say, "That's not me," concluding that they weren't meant to be creative. On the other hand, if I told them to simply be less restrictive in their questioning, most people would conclude, "I can do that, show me how."

The process of imagining and asking "what if" go hand-in-hand.

Here's my final selling point on what-if questions. The process of imagining and asking "what if" go hand-in-hand. When you want to imagine something, you ask "what if?" When you ask "what if," you begin to imagine. There is no way to disconnect the two, which is what makes what-if questions so valuable.

When you imagine, as Einstein did with his thought experiments, or as King does when generating story ideas, you're visiting new vantage points that are the key to creative reframing and seeing new ideas. It's for this reason the words *imaginative* and *creative* serve as synonyms for each other. The words live as kin because imagining is a technique used to build creativity . . . and what-if questions serve as your doorway to imagination.

Taking a STAB: The Twenty Questions Stimulator

If coming up with twenty new questions is tough, regardless of whether they start with "what if" or something else, that's because you're trained to think and ask realistic questions. And within the set of realistic questions you typically consider, you're trained to hone in on one, not diverge into twenty. What I'm teaching you represents a change in your approach, which means a new discipline for you to learn.

If you're posed with a problem and struggling to generate what-if questions, here's a surefire stimulator to get you started—the STAB exercise. I've named it the STAB for three reasons. First, it's a handy acronym to remember and incorporate into your life or your corporate culture, much the way the SWOT analysis (strengths, weaknesses, opportunities, and threats) is a default exercise for companies or organizations doing competitive strategy work. Think of the STAB as a SWOT-like, go-to exercise but instead of generating strategic insights, you'll use it to generate lots of questions (unlike the SWOT, the STAB isn't a true matrix, but the quadrant-like arrangement makes it easier to visualize).

Second, the phrase "take a stab" captures precisely the attitude I want you to have as you go through it. You're saying, "I'll give this a try, and we'll see what we see." That's the reality of asking lots of questions. Some will produce terrific ideas and some will produce nothing in the way of new thinking. Recognizing that ahead of time will keep you from feeling like you're failing when some of your questions fall flat.

Finally, STAB serves as an acronym for four of the most common types of questions I pose in my ideation sessions. These are questions that:

Change the **S**ix *Circumstances* of a problem or opportunity.

Change the **T**raits of a problem.

Challenge the **A**ssumptions we make about a problem.

Challenge the **B**arriers that keep us from solving a problem.

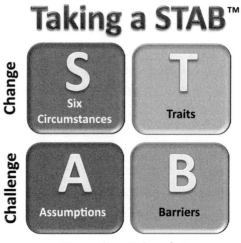

Taking a STAB™

Change — S Six Circumstances | T Traits

Challenge — A Assumptions | B Barriers

Question Stimulator

Most problems, regardless of industry, regardless of profession, tend to come with these four aspects built in: six circumstances, traits, assumptions, and barriers. But you need to know that the results of the STAB will vary significantly from problem to problem. Coming up with new kinds of hammers is a very different creative challenge than figuring out how to solve childhood obesity. The STAB will work; it's just that it will work differently depending on the nature of your problem. For example, if you're trying to redesign a hammer, a hammer clearly has traits that you can change. If you're trying to solve obesity, defining the traits of your problem will be more difficult than listing your assumptions. The point to remember: the STAB is a question *stimulator* and depending on the problem, some quadrants will stimulate better than others and some may not stimulate at all. Enough already, let's take a STAB!

Six Circumstances (Who, What, Why, Where, When, How)

What I call the Six Circumstances appear in many different ways, with a multitude of uses outside of creativity. Also known as the Six Ws (or Five Ws and one H), it's a basic template for information-gathering among journalists, researchers, and even police investigators. Unlike journalism or detective work, where your objective is to fill in or uncover the Six Ws, our objective is to change them; our problem already comes with its own starting circumstances. Only by changing the original circumstances of our problem can we trigger questions that will lead to new places to find ideas.

This quadrant of the STAB is the most fun because it allows you to roam the most freely. Start by writing *who, what, why, when, where*, and *how* down the left side of your notepad. From there, focus for a few minutes on each one and generate questions to the right. Just by moving these elements of your problem into working memory, you'll begin to "see" new questions. (This might be a good moment to read the upcoming sidetrack "How to Stimulate Questions.") I generated the "What if Jay Leno ran our shareholder meeting" question through this step of the STAB exercise. I simply focused on the *who* and imagined changing that part of my creative challenge in a provocative way. Who's running the meeting? Who's speaking at the meeting? Who's planning the meeting?

From there, I imagined (there's that word again) different scenarios and converted my thinking into what-if questions. What if kids ran it? What if retirees ran it? What if shareholders ran it? What if nobody ran it? What if an entertainer ran it? What if Jay Leno ran it? All of these take my mind different places, but I settled on the Leno question for my example because it seemed creatively promising. In real life, I would take the time to ponder every what-if question for the ideas they produce. So should you.

The other five circumstances all work in a similar manner. All you have to do is focus on one circumstance of your problem at a time and allow yourself to drift from the original parameters of the problem and think, "What if?"

Taking a STAB™

Six Circumstances

How can we make shareholder meetings more engaging?

Circumstance	Sample What-if Question
Change: Who something is happening to or who is doing something.	What if Jay Leno ran the meeting?
Change: What is happening.	What if new products could speak for themselves?
Change: Why they are doing something or why something is happening.	What if we made annual meetings a way to make employees excited?
Change: When it is happening.	What if we held it on New Year's Eve?
Change: Where it is happening.	What if the meeting was everywhere at once?
Change: How it is happening.	What if the meeting was like a movie?

When I think about *what* as it relates to shareholder meetings, I think about what CEOs talk about. New products introduced over the past year, or due to be introduced, are always on the agenda. It's an example of a *what*. As I think about making these meetings more engaging, I imagine the question, "What if new products could talk?" Of course they can't, but what if they could? This leads to the idea of short videos where each new product tells its own life story, in its own voice, about how it was conceived and shaped by the company's ingenious employees. Giving new products their own voice and personality is a much different level of engagement than simply introducing them.

The *when* led to New Year's Eve—not a good time for a shareholder meeting, but certainly a time when most people are engaged. During bad years, New Year's Eve parties are a time of resolutions, of wiping the slate clean. During our bad years, could we make restless shareholders less anxious and more interested if we presented our plans for the year not as strategies, but as resolutions? Strategies sound boring and expected and changeable. Resolutions suggest a cleaning of the slate—a good thing after a crappy year.

The *why* led me to challenge why we have these meetings in the first place and what they are intended to accomplish. I wonder: "What if we used shareholder meetings to make our employees more excited, not just our shareholders?" When I think about this particular question, no ideas come to mind. At least not for me, at least not right away. A dry hole. Move on. Some questions are like that.

The *how* makes me think, "How might we tell the story?" This leads me to imagine, "What if we showed a movie instead?" While showing a movie is probably not a realistic solution, it does make me think about a creative process where we figure out which movie—past or present— best represents our year. Perhaps we show clips of that movie (with approval, of course) to demonstrate key points. Perhaps we use the movie as an ongoing metaphor. Perhaps we think about what movie genre our year most resembles. Was the year a feel-good movie, a mystery, an action flick, a disaster film, or a sexy merger? Can we construct our presentation to fit this genre?

Some of these ideas were good ones, some not so good. That's typical of the creative process. Yet all the questions led me to new places. What's even better—your questions will be different from mine, as will your ideas. Add more people, you add even more questions and end up with even more ideas, some of which will be winners.

Traits

Traits are the characteristics of your problem or the characteristics of the focus of your problem. For example, if we're trying to generate new kinds of hammers, hammers are clearly the focus. Certain traits are generally true about a hammer. For starters, it has one head, the head faces out, and the head is hard. If you were focusing on a school, it also has certain traits: individual classrooms, organized by grades, led by a teacher, and so on.

Listing your problem's traits, then thinking about altering them, can lead to some powerful what-if questions. Let's take the hammer for a few swings and try to come up with some new product ideas. To keep it simple, let's just focus on one part of a hammer: the head.

Let's take the trait "a hammer has one head." When you focus on an individual trait and think about changing it, what-if questions leap from your brain. What if a hammer had more than one head? From this question, ideas can leap forth just as quickly. Think about a hammer with more than one head. What do you envision? How literally did you see it? I envision a hammer where you can attach a wide range of hammerheads—not unlike electric screwdrivers with interchangeable heads. Rather than owning three or four hammers, you could own just one with multiple heads, each attaching to a comfortable, durable, and extremely high-end handle. You could even give that handle a lifetime warranty, thereby assuring that all future heads will be purchased for your hammer.

Taking a STAB™

Traits

What kinds of new product ideas can we create for hammers or hammering nails?

Traits	What-if Questions	Ideas
Has one head	What if it had multiple heads?	Hammer with interchangeable, screw-in heads. The only hammer you'll ever need!
The head faces out	What if the head faced up?	Head can move to different positions so hammer can get into tight areas. Make electric?
The head is hard	What if the head was soft?	Hammer Helper. Holds nail for you and enlarges nail head. Never miss nail; never hit thumb!

Think about the trait "a hammer's head faces out." What if a hammer had a head that faced up? Can you picture that in your mind? Can you begin to imagine what a hammer shaped like that might be good for? What about pounding nails in tight areas difficult to reach with the standard striking motion? A hammer with a head that faces up allows you to hammer in more of a stabbing motion than a swinging motion—maybe not as efficient, but certainly useful if the nail is located in a space where that's the only way to strike it. Perhaps you could make it more efficient by providing a power source to the hammer so it works like a mini jackhammer?

When you think about changing traits, you can either alter them (multiple heads versus one) or in some cases, think of their opposite. For example, thinking the opposite of the trait "hammerheads are hard" leads to the provocative and reality-suspending question: What if hammerheads were soft? Again, think about what would happen if you hammered a hard nail with a soft-headed hammer. Can you picture the result in your mind? A soft head wouldn't move the nail; it would just envelop and surround the nail head. A bad thing? Maybe not. That makes the head of the nail a temporarily bigger target, which leads to a completely different idea. Something you hold in your left hand (if right-handed) that goes over the nail to create a bigger striking surface so you can then whack the hell out of it with a conventional hammer in your right hand. Then you'd never miss another nail! I didn't invent a new hammer here, but I did just invent the first Hammer Helper.

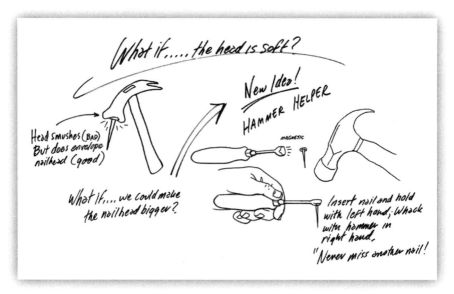

Whiteboard Tip: Sometimes one "what if" will trigger a new "what if." Let it!

Challenging traits can immediately lead you to new ideas—as the multiple heads question did—or it can take your brain to a new place. From that new place, you can jump to a new idea. For example, the "what if" of a soft hammerhead didn't lead me directly to a new idea. Instead, when I pictured the hammer in use, I saw it surrounding the nail, creating something that looked like a larger nail head. That made me think, "What if we could make the nail head bigger so you never miss hitting the nail on the head (and consequently, never hit your thumb)?"

That's the power of challenging traits. When I initially thought of new hammers, I was thinking of making a different hammer; I hadn't even considered the possibility of inventing something that made my current hammer work better. You won't either unless you open yourself up to this type of unrestricted questioning.

Assumptions

Nothing limits our thinking more than the assumptions we make. What's worse is that most assumptions are so ingrained into the problem (and our own thinking), that we don't even realize we're making them. We accept them as truths, but assumptions aren't truths; they're merely beliefs we hold to be as good as true. Surfacing these assumptions and then challenging them usually triggers some truly great questions and breakthrough thinking. But be aware, your questions will challenge beliefs held as fundamentally true, so some of your resulting what-if questions may sound ridiculous when you first think of them. Just give them a chance.

For example, in education we hold as incontestable truth that we provide instruction during school and do homework after school. The notion of flipping these sounds absurd. Yet the success of the Khan Academy videos is prompting some innovative schools, including one here in my town, to give it a try. Likewise, football coaches assume that onside kicks must be used sparingly, as an element of surprise or a last-ditch effort in the final minutes. Yet, Kevin Kelley, a football coach in Arkansas, directs his high-school team to onside kick every time, a seemingly absurd idea that challenges the long-held assumption. In one astounding game, his now nationally ranked Pulaski Academy team forged ahead 29-0 before the other team touched the ball!

For our practice example, let's switch industries to hotels and switch objectives to focus on value. Pretend you're the vice president of operations at a mid-priced hotel chain. Your objective is to figure out how to deliver more value to your guests. Since value is often defined as "what you get" divided by "what you pay," there are many different ways to improve a hotel's value equation. You can reduce the "what you pay" part by figuring out how to drive costs out of the system, perhaps by eliminating the things guests don't value, reducing staff, or streamlining operations. Or you can focus on the "what you get part" by replacing services and amenities with different ones that return more bang for the buck. Or you can impact guests' *perception* of value—for example, giving guests the feeling that they're only paying for the stuff they need. So, recognizing that value creation is a broad objective that we can achieve in many different ways, let's pose our beginning objective: "In what ways might we (a hotel operator) improve value or perception of value for our guests?"

Like the other quadrants, the first step is to create a list, in this case some assumptions about your problem. Our what-if questions will spring from these assumptions. Since most of us have stayed at mid-level hotels at some point (such as Hampton Inns or Embassy Suites), we probably know enough to list some assumptions. I've filled out the table below with some assumptions and the what-if questions these assumptions triggered for me. You can write in some of your own questions, as well. Also, if you want, write down any ideas these questions trigger in the idea column. Go ahead. I've put in a few of my own in the last column to seed the cloud.

Taking a STAB™

Assumptions

In what ways can we (hotel operator) improve our perception of value for our guests?

Assumptions	What-if Questions	Ideas
Housekeeping matters	What if you only paid for what you valued?	Room comes with "2 side dishes" (like a value menu). Only pay for what you use.
Hotels need staff	What if we could run a hotel with no staff?	Own a permanent key card that's activated when needed (similar to unstaffed fitness clubs).
Hotel rooms have bathrooms	What if people shared bathrooms?	Create male and female only hotels (similar to health clubs).
All guests are different	What if we grouped guests by similar needs?	Quiet floor contract (like honors dorms at college).

Challenging the assumption that people care about housekeeping leads me to wonder, "What if guests only paid for what they valued?" This question prompts an idea-link from a different industry. Recall how value menus work in some fast-food restaurants. For a fixed amount of money, you get to pick a set number of items from a list of possible options. Or think about how sit-down restaurants give you a choice of two sides with your meal. In our hotel chain example, instead of choosing two side dishes or two items from the value menu, you choose two amenities from the hotel menu—fitness room, Internet, housekeeping, or breakfast. When you pick and use just two, you get the room at a low rate. To get extra amenities, you pay an added price. In this way, guests feel like they are only paying for the amenities they're using. Think it sounds absurd? There are lots of guests who won't go to a hotel with a pool because they feel like they're paying for a pool they'll never use. If I had told you ten years ago that someday you'd pay twenty-five dollars to check your bag on a plane trip, you'd call me crazy. Some value-based hotels may head in the same direction someday. If they do, don't blame me.

Note that this question uncovered an idea-link from another category, restaurants. Some of my other questions in the table did the same. Depending on the question, they made me think of what has worked for fitness clubs (no-staff clubs like Anytime Fitness and gender-specific clubs like Curves for Women) and what has worked for colleges (the creation of honors floors where everyone agrees to certain restrictions). The question about sharing bathrooms led me to the idea of a male-only hotel (which I rejected), which in turn led me to the idea of a female-only hotel, where women would perhaps feel safer. Is this a value idea? It is if women would be willing to pay a premium for the same thing they get at other hotels, without the possibility of smarmy, martini-reeking businessmen leering at them on the way to their rooms.

When I asked the question about grouping guests by similarity, it triggered an idea-link I recently made while my son and I toured colleges. Some colleges attract top students by offering specific dorm options for honor students—a nicer room, provided they agree to certain quiet hours. Could you also create a quiet floor of a hotel, where all guests agree to be in their rooms by 11:00 p.m. so as not to wake other guests with ice crashing into metal buckets, doors slamming, or elevators dinging? If I have a speech the next day, I might spring for an extra fifteen dollars a night just to make sure I get a good night's sleep. Anybody who's ever been awakened from a deep sleep by some idiot stumbling in at 2:00 a.m., then had to face a brutally long day on three hours' sleep, understands the appeal of a quiet floor. Come to think of it, some nights I'd pay an extra $25 for the assurance that it won't happen. That's added revenue in the hotel's pocket for doing nothing but grouping similar people together, an idea that's been used by colleges for decades, perhaps longer.

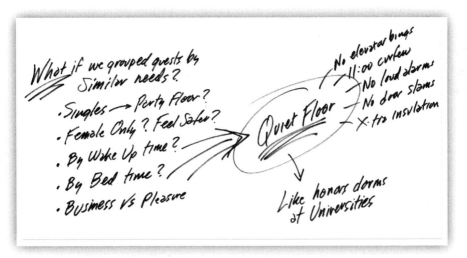

Whiteboard Tip: Write down all the thoughts your "what if" triggers. Seeing them together allows you to connect them into a new idea.

Note that in the process of challenging assumptions, you may also end up challenging traits, or even wondering how a trait is different from an assumption. Don't worry—thinking about something as a trait in one quadrant and an assumption in a different quadrant will lead you to different places. If we had listed the traits of a hotel, we might say that having *one pool* is a trait of mid-level hotels. That mid-level hotels *must have a pool* is an assumption. If I change the trait, I might ask, "What if hotels had a pool for every guest?" That leads me to imagine having a cluster of hot tubs at slightly different temperatures, instead of one big 78-degree indoor pool—something that might appeal more to business travelers and ultimately take up less space. Wording the question this way makes me think of a different execution of the idea of a pool.

Challenging the assumption that we have pools with, "What if we eliminated all pools and replaced them with something else?" might lead me to question why we have pools in the first place. If it's for family entertainment, would families prefer to have an assortment of family-friendly activities in the same space? Let's say a Wii station, a laser-tag area, and a Wiffle ball court? And when no one is using them, it costs the hotel operator nothing; not the case with a pool, which constantly gurgles away electricity and churns through chlorine.

So again, don't sweat it if some of your assumptions challenge the very traits you listed in the previous STAB quadrant. Trait-based questions and assumption-based questions lead you to different places. The idea of replacing the pool with an activity court is a very different idea from converting one big swimming pool into multiple hot tubs. That's because your trait-based "what ifs" *change* what the pool is like; assumption-based "what ifs" *challenge* its very existence.

Barriers

Barriers are easier to find than assumptions. Whereas assumptions lurk under the surface, often unnoticed, you bump into barriers every day. That's why the barrier quadrant is probably the easiest one to fill. Barriers usually come to mind quickly, especially if you've got some help from fellow team members. Pessimistic team members are especially helpful at this stage (provided you can make them go away in the later stages). They're always moaning about why something can't be done, making them life's barrier-generating machines. This is the perfect time to turn them on and let them vent! (Note: If you recognize yourself as overly pessimistic, try to learn to convert your natural pessimism into what-if questions. While there is significant value in finding problems and barriers others overlook, if you do nothing but point out barriers, you slowly erode the hope and patience of those you work with. You become a downer. You'll add much more value to a team if you also offer what-if questions related to those same barriers. Then you'll be a *creative* pessimist.)

For the final example, we'll move away from business and take on a stubborn societal problem: childhood obesity. I'm no expert on the subject, but for purposes of the exercise, I'll make some educated guesses about the barriers and try not to offend anyone in the process.

You'll find that what-if questions come to you quickly and naturally as you look over your list of barriers. Also notice that in some cases the "what if" you generate will actually be the idea. For example, "What if there were a group of people who understood obese kids?" is really more of an idea than a question. Sometimes, just focusing on a barrier will lead directly to an idea. That's okay. Keep the question as part of your list of twenty because it may lead to further ideas.

Taking a STAB™

Barriers

In what ways can we solve or minimize childhood obesity?

Barriers to solving the problem	What-if Questions	Ideas
Parents can perpetuate the problem by feeding their kids treats as a reward or expression of love.	What if we could show parents the impact of extra treats over time?	Do computer simulation of how their kids "expand" with one extra treat per week over a twenty-year period.
Families struggling with obesity can lose sense for what is normal.	What if we could quantify what normal behavior is?	Develop the "BMI" of behavior (OLI = Obesity Likelihood index).
People who try to help obese kids often don't understand them.	What if there were a group of people who understood obese kids and could relate to them?	Enlist adults who struggled with weight as children to help obese kids, not personal trainers who were never overweight.

You may have other questions that are less suggestive of an idea and are more dependent on where the question takes your brain. When I asked, "What if we could quantify what is normal behavior?" I immediately thought of another form of quantification, the Body Mass Index (BMI). This led me to the realization that while the BMI is useful, it only measures how bad the problem is once it's a problem. The real need is to make people aware of how bad their behavior is, because it's the behavior that leads to the problem. The BMI is like a stick that tells you how high a flood is; I want a measurement that will help prevent the flood in the first place.

So what if parents answer a survey about their parenting behaviors, beliefs, and attitudes that generated a number—let's call it the Obesity Likelihood Index, or OLI. The OLI tells you how likely the cumulative effect of your parenting style, nutritional knowledge, and family eating habits will ultimately contribute to obesity in your children. Using this type of index puts the responsibility more on the parents—the adults in the problem—and less on the kids. And it catches the problem before it's a problem. If this type of index doesn't already exist, it should.

Taking a STAB on Your Own

In the demonstration, I changed the problem for each quadrant just to maintain variety. When you use STAB in real life, you'll have one problem that you'll work through all four quadrants. The next time you have a problem you need to quickly get creative about, do the following:

1. Take five minutes to think of and write down as many questions as you can, in whatever format comes to you naturally. If some questions don't come to you as what-if questions, write them down anyway. At the end of the five-minute period, convert all questions into a what-if format, if possible. If you can't, leave it as is. This initial list represents the questions that naturally arise from your current working memory of the problem.

2. Print out the four pages of the STAB quadrants from TheNewCreativity.com (under Extras). If you can't access the quadrants online, simply recreate each table from the STAB quadrant by hand. Doing it manually will take less than a minute and allow you to use whatever size paper you want.

3. Write your problem statement at the top of each page. If you're doing it by hand, add the words *who, what, why, when, where,* and *how* on the Six Circumstances page. List the traits of the problem (or the subject of your problem) on the Traits page. List all the assumptions you make about the problem on the Assumptions page. List all the barriers you face in solving this problem on the Barriers page.

4. As you go down the lists you just created, spend about five minutes per page to generate what-if questions and record them on each page. There's no limit to the number of questions you can generate; just be sure to get at least twenty, and be sure to cover each quadrant.

5. Once you have all your questions, read through them one at a time, allowing each question to generate new questions, new directions, or new ideas. Capture individual ideas on index cards, one idea per card so you can separate your questions from your ideas. Note that some questions will take you to ideas, while others will end with nothing to show for your effort. Again, that's why it's called taking a STAB.

6. If you're doing this as a group, swap questions and see what ideas the same questions trigger in other people, or read through all the questions as a group. I've found the stage of question generation works best individually, whereas the idea-generation stage works best as a group.

Using the STAB prompts will help whenever you're having trouble coming up with lots of questions on your own, but I always recommend that you try to come up with your own questions first, before using the prompts. Getting into the habit of asking your own questions builds your questioning muscle more than relying on the prompts, much the way lifting free weights adds strength faster than an exercise machine that guides and assists your body.

Also, remember that some quadrants will work and others won't, depending on the problem. But sometimes just one question in an otherwise unproductive quadrant will lead to the biggest idea. Try them all, but don't fret if one quadrant is really difficult. Every problem is different.

Finally, don't limit yourself to STAB-generated questions. Any question that changes or challenges some aspect of your problem is a potentially revealing one. The STAB is just a great tool to generate many of them.

With the what-if format in your head, Twenty Questions as your goal, and the STAB in your back pocket, you'll soon be generating revealing questions with the best of them.

• • •

I've purposely excluded from the STAB exercise an absolutely killer kind of what-if question, because you won't find these kinds of "what ifs" in every profession. But in the professions that have them, they hold tremendous creative value. They're next.

SIDETRACK: How to Stimulate Questions

If you're wondering why it's difficult to just sit down and crank out questions, blame your working memory. While conflicting theories exist about what working memory is and how it operates, most agree on two things: 1) working memory is used to do complex tasks like reasoning and comprehension, and 2) your brain can only hold limited amounts of data in working memory. It's the inherent limitation of working memory that inhibits our ability to generate lots of questions on command. It also explains why the STAB helps you generate more.

Just as ideas need the raw material of idea-links, questions feed off the stuff in your working memory. The problem with working memory is you can't expand the amount it holds. Think of it like a ten-by-ten-foot storage shed with immovable walls. Want to put new things in? Better take something else out. The new stuff indiscriminately pushes out the old. So you can't give your brain more working memory, you can only give it different working memory. Think of the STAB as giving your working memory a conveyor belt of new stuff to work from. The more new stuff you push through, the more questions you'll generate.

You know your problem's barriers and traits; it's just that they're not in working memory until you pull them there. As soon as you go through the STAB, you pull barriers, traits, and other facts into working memory and thereby trigger new questions, almost like magic. For example, if I ask you to come up with questions about the atmosphere, you'll no doubt have enough working memory to come up with some. If I ask you to list traits of the sky, you might come up with "blue." This triggers the question, "Why is the sky blue?" If the sky's color wasn't initially in your working memory about the atmosphere, this question never happens, even though you know the sky is blue.

That's also why reading a research report or hearing others talk about your problem will trigger new questions. Each bring different stimuli into your working memory. That's why, in addition to doing the STAB, I recommend reading about and exposing yourself to as much as you can about your problem, recording questions as they come up. It's also why I recommend you do the STAB on paper, ideally on as big a sheet as possible. Having your six circumstances, traits, assumptions, and barriers in front of you, on paper, artificially expands your working memory. Kind of like renting a few more ten-by-ten sheds of working memory. If it's there in front of you, you don't have to remember it. You can simply enter the new shed and let the stuff inside it trigger new questions.

So read reports. Find related articles. Talk to colleagues. Take a STAB. Don't let the limits of working memory limit the number of questions you ask.

The Old Creativity	The New Creativity
Become more playful.	Become less restricted in your questioning.

10

Strategic What Ifs

*All men can see these tactics whereby I conquer, but
what none can see
is the strategy out of which victory is evolved.*

—SUN TZU, CHINESE MILITARY STRATEGIST

*The best CEOs I know are teachers, and at the core of
what they teach is strategy.*

—MICHAEL PORTER, MANAGEMENT CONSULTANT

If I told you about a great idea I came up with in the shower,
you'd probably call me creative. But if I gave you the exact
same idea, and then explained that I had simply applied a
framework I'd recently memorized from a book, you'd say
I'm strategic.

We call people strategic when their ideas are reinforced by some manner of logic, unlike the "out-there" or "from-the-blue" ideas we normally classify as creative. But a great idea is a great idea, regardless of its backstory or the person delivering it. Strategic people are creative, even if their creativity springs from a source that can seem, well, boring.

Strategic people are creative, even if their creativity springs from a source that can seem boring.

If the source is boring, the results are not. Strategic people are the ones who somehow see tough problems with great clarity, when all the other people in the room are spinning their wheels. For these rare types, the facts and disparate pieces of data seem to magically align to form a clear picture from a muddled mess. Suddenly, out of the blue, they say, "I think we should do x for y reason," leaving the rest in the group kicking themselves and asking, "Why can't I be that smart?! Why didn't I see that?!"

Great strategists excel at deconstructing problems, generating options, then skillfully selecting the best one. One of the ways they generate options is to see problems through a strategic lens. To say "a" lens makes it sound like there's one big magic lens. On the contrary, strategic types carry a sack of lenses, putting them on and taking them off faster than an optometrist can say, "Better A, or better B?" Over time, they gain an instinctive sense for which sets of lenses are most likely to uncover a workable solution.

"Seeing" Bing

Let's try on some strategic lenses with a case study. Microsoft's new search engine, Bing, garnered a thirty-percent share of the search engine category in an impressively short period of time (based on March 2011 U.S. market share data).[55] How did they do that? And where did the idea itself come from?

To invent Bing, we're going to learn another kind of "what if." To understand how it works you'll need to take a new job, at least temporarily, and travel in time before Bing was invented. First, close your eyes and imagine you're in a gleaming office building in the Pacific Northwest. Your new position: director of strategy with Microsoft. Your task: figure out a creative and profitable way to enter the search business, taking on the industry monster, Google. You've just settled into your chair. Fourth floor window office. Blank piece of paper. Pen in hand. Door closed.

Where do you start? Where will the creative ideas come from? How can you go from owning this nearly impossible task to owning a creative new solution? Sound daunting? For those who think strategically, seeing creative options emerge from tough, complex problems such as these is simpler than you might guess.

One immediate angle is to think of the challenge in terms of strategic warfare. One company is attacking the other, right? For the strategic thinker, that brings to mind competition books like *Blue Ocean Strategy*, *The Art of War*, *The Innovator's Solution*, and *Marketing Warfare*.[56] Now, all your strategic lenses associated with these books emerge as questions—as different ways to reframe the problem. So what exactly is a strategic lens and how is it used to find new ideas?

Let's use the marketing classic, *Marketing Warfare*, by Ries and Trout as an example. In it, the authors give you their prescription for winning competitive battles based on the principles from the 1832 military classic *On War* by Karl von Clausewitz.[57] If you were to extract the book's principles and think of each of them as different what-if questions, you could look at any competitive situation and ask, "What if we attacked the weakness in Google's strength?" or "What if we attacked on a narrow front? Then what would we see?" In other words, what ideas does this line of questioning reveal to me? In this way, Ries and Trout's strategic principles from *Marketing Warfare* act like lenses. When you look at your problem through them, you see different aspects of your "battle." This makes strategic lenses like any other what-if question, except they are strategic in nature.

From *Blue Ocean Strategy* you might pose the questions, "What if we eliminated a factor from our offering?" or "What if we raised a factor by joining forces with someone else?" From *The Innovator's Solutions*, you posit "What if we created a Low-End or New-Market Disruption?" Each strategic lens causes you to consider the problem differently, and in the process, see different strategic options. But be patient—the first six lenses you try on may lead nowhere. The seventh may be the magic lens.

All of these books about competition lead to different ideas, but if you look at your problem through some of the *Marketing Warfare* lenses—create a new mental category, find the weakness in the strength, and attack on a narrow front—you'll see one possible source of inspiration for the idea that became Bing. First, what if we attacked the weakness in Google's strength? What might we see? The strength of a great search engine like Google is its ability to return lots of results. In fact, Google's search powers are so complete that there's even a drinking game called Stump Google. Pick two or three words and see who can come up with the fewest search results (I just gave it a try and "McRib, sawdust, screwdriver" spit out 2,660 results). A search engine that returns massive results for each query is a great resource . . . unless you need to make a decision. When making a quick decision, pages and pages of results—especially irrelevant results—leave you paralyzed. By focusing their product and positioning on the decision-making aspect of search, Bing exploited this inherent weakness—the weakness in Google's strength.

Then, they created a new mental category—what Ries and Trout and von Clausewitz call Flanking Warfare. Rather than just become another search engine, they'd break out from the clutter by becoming first in something new, based upon an inherent Google weakness. Bing called itself the world's first Decision Engine. With that coinage, there are now search engines, and there are decision engines, an element of the idea easily seen through the "create a new category" lens.

Returning to a *Blue Ocean Strategy* lens and asking the question, "What if we raised a factor by partnering with someone else?" causes your mind to search for other companies who can make your search results more decision-friendly (again, the factor we're raising is the ability to make a quick, informed decision). As you think about how people decide, you would no doubt learn, or intuitively know, that most people (ninety percent, to be precise) seek advice from family and friends as part of the decision-making process. Now, looking through the lens of "partnership seeking," can you think of a company Bing might align with to provide family and friend referrals? Some way to know which restaurants your friends and family "like"? That's right, Facebook.[58] Try Bing and you'll see how they leverage this partnership to speed decision making.

Whether Bing ultimately beats Google or not is beside the point. (In fact, until their recent partnership with Facebook, I had my doubts that Microsoft had convincingly demonstrated how their search product is better for making decisions.) The point is that looking through strategic lenses can unlock great ideas, even though the process itself may seem dull, formulaic, and uninspired.

Looking Through Strategic Lenses Is a Type of Creative Reframing

With each lens we looked through in the Bing example, we saw something different because we strategically reframed the problem each time. In that way, looking through a strategic lens is like any other kind of reframing question, only they're strategic in nature. The more strategic lenses you can try on, the more ways you creatively reframe your problem. And as you've already seen, the more ways you can reframe, the greater your odds of unlocking the idea that makes everyone else in the room green with envy.

When you put on a strategic lens, you're essentially asking: "What if we looked at the problem through this way of thinking? What new solutions or approaches might we see?" From this point on, whenever you see a strategic principle or strategic framework, I want you to think of it as a potentially killer what-if question that you can return to again and again. But seeing these strategic "what ifs" is only the first step in owning them.

A Strategy toward Becoming More Strategically Creative

If you find strategic people's approach to creativity dull, prepare for more dullness: Part of their secret is nothing more than memorization and hard work. For example, lots of people have read *Marketing Warfare*. But few have committed the principles to memory. And exceedingly few can both recite the principles *and* tell you how they work. You see, you can't put a lens on until you own it. And you can't own it until you remember it. When strategic people are being strategic, part of what they're doing is simply cycling through all the frameworks and principles stored in their heads, asking themselves, "What do I see if we did this?" until they land on an idea or solution that seems like a good one. It's all happening in their heads so you never see it.

If you want to become strategically creative yourself, once again, you'll have to commit to some hard work. Strategic people don't just stumble across their strategic skills. They weren't born with them. They did the work to extract these lenses and implant them permanently in their brains. If you want to join their ranks, you'll need to change. One way to do so is to begin noticing the strategic successes around you, like new companies, new products, or new approaches that have taken off, some of which I briefly mentioned in the Business Model Idea-Links section. Then analyze what they did strategically to help them succeed. The result of your analysis becomes a new strategic lens to look through. Another way to start accumulating strategic lenses is to read differently.

Strategic reading

Too often we think of reading as a passive exercise. We let the words rush over us but few actually stick. Strategic people read books differently; they make reading a hunting expedition, a search for the strategic principles they know will have utility later. As they hunt the principles down, they write them down, mark them with a Post-it® flag, or commit them to memory.

Some years back, I gave a speech to a major corporation and during the speech, wanted to demonstrate how little information our brains actually retain from the books we read if we don't consciously work at it. To prove my point, I asked how many had read *The Tipping Point* by Malcolm Gladwell, which had been published two years earlier.[59] All twenty-three people raised their hands. Perfect. Who could name or explain the three main principles of *The Tipping Point* (The Law of the Few, The Power of Context, Stickiness)? All hands dropped. How about two principles? Hands still down. How about one of the principles? Again, no hands. Finally, one person from the audience, ever so slowly, raised his hand. Yes! Someone remembered one of the main principles. Well, not really. Instead, I got a sheepish confession: "Jim, it gets worse."

"How could it get worse?" I asked.

"The author spoke at our company earlier this month."

If you think about it, strategic frameworks found in books like *The Tipping Point* are multiple idea-links organized into some kind of structure. That structure—and the name for the structure—make it sound bigger and more important than the individual idea-links. They are called things like Gladwell's Three Rules of Epidemics, or Ries and Trout's 22 Immutable Laws, or The Principles of Marketing Warfare, or Porter's Five Forces, or the BCG Matrix, or the Heath brothers' SUCCESS acronym from *Made to Stick*. But deep down, what's behind all of them is analysis. The author has analyzed countless situations and figured out what frequently works and why—that's our definition of an idea-link. Then the author extracts it, makes it succinct, combines it with other idea-links he or she has discovered, and ties them all together under some memorable and important-sounding name. By the time it has all been packaged by the author and the publisher, it no longer looks like a collection of idea-links. But that's what strategic frameworks are. They're simply strategic idea-links neatly organized into a framework or list.

Business books—if done well—burst with these strategic idea-links because that's what good authors do. They explain things and why they work. Authors do the thinking and the analysis for us, and hand us idea-links in easy-to-remember and easy-to-use frameworks. But if we never go through the exercise of finding and remembering these frameworks, reading business books is a waste of time, at least from the standpoint of improving your creativity. If you're going to read a business book like *Marketing Warfare* and not pull out even one strategic nugget you can use later, really, why even bother? You might as well spend your time reading suspense novels—you won't get creative, but at least you'll enjoy the read.

If you're truly committed to becoming more creative, you have to commit to reading books differently. Your objective is not to finish the book and say you read it. Your objective is to extract as many strategic gems as you can and say you remember them. In fact, you're much better off skimming a book to find the meaty parts, or reading select chapters to pull out and memorize one framework, than to read an entire book, say that you read it, and leave with nothing to use later. And if, after a few chapters, a book seems barren of usable strategic principles or frameworks, put it down and sell it on eBay. Your time is far more valuable than the $24.99 you spent on the book.

Remember, you're on the hunt for strategic principles and frameworks you can turn into what-if questions. And when you're reading a book, they're often right under your nose. When you stop reading books to finish them and start reading to accumulate strategic principles and frameworks to look through as lenses, they'll jump off the page and join your ever-growing stockpile. Write them down and store them somewhere. Then, next time you have a challenging problem, go through your list, thinking of them as what-if questions. Before long you'll learn how to cycle through these lenses without the list. Then you too will become one of these strategic-creative wonders.

Starting your own collection of lenses

I can't tell you what books to read for every profession. I'm a marketing and new products guy, as you've seen with some of the books I've used to find different lenses. But if you want to start grabbing some for yourself, here's a quick shortcut. Think of two or three of the most gifted strategists you know in your profession and ask them what books they'd recommend. Or even better, find out what lenses they try on when they're problem-solving and where they got them in the first place. You'll find most strategic types are more than willing to share their secrets, though sometimes their lenses are so ingrained into their thinking, they may forget they had to acquire them from somewhere years ago. Explain what you mean by lenses (or frameworks), then give them time. Eventually, they'll remember.

Or get together with a colleague or two and think about all the strategy books and mental frameworks that relate to your functional area. Rather than leaving them on a bookshelf, why not assemble a team and distill and gather all the relevant frameworks in one place, so you can all use them? Think deeply about areas where you need to become more creative in your job. You may decide, for example, that you need to find ways to make your messages more impactful and memorable, whether it's for advertising, public relations, or teaching a group of high-school students. If that's the case, there's a book for that: *Made to Stick*, by the Heath brothers. In it, you'll find a slick acronym they call SUCCES, with each letter of the acronym serving as a different lens you can try on. Trying to get creative about writing a more compelling press release? Try on the Heath's Unexpected lens and see what you see. Or their Concrete lens. Cycling through all six lenses gives you six more creative ways to think about your problem.

When you find great frameworks like SUCCES, extract them into a succinct, usable form and put them in a convenient place so you can refer to them later. Early in my marketing career, I surrounded myself with a collection of books, each with an assortment of Post-it® flags sticking out of key pages. When I was searching for an idea,

I might thumb through these books, flag by flag, to see what inspiration they'd trigger and remind myself of useful strategic principles. Do this enough times and the frameworks and principles become part of you—the books are no longer needed.

Strategic lenses are there for the taking. You just have to care enough to acquire them. Once you feel like you have a good foundation within your profession, you're ready for the next step of lens collection.

Borrowing lenses from other fields

When companies hire organization development and human resources (HR) design consultants Mary Jenkins and Howard Stanton to redesign their human resource systems (such as incentive systems), they do so because Jenkins and Stanton help them see solutions that were previously not apparent. So what do Jenkins and Stanton see that others do not? The better question is what allows Jenkins and Stanton to see what others in their field do not?

While at General Motors, Jenkins studied under Dr. W. Edwards Deming—the father of the post-war industrial revival in Japan, and later, the leader of the quality movement in the United States. Jenkins's deep immersion in Deming's work implanted in her a certain set of lenses from outside the world of human resources, through which she looks at problems inside HR.

Because she wears the lenses of a quality practitioner, Jenkins sees HR topics such as compensation, appraisal, and attendance policy differently than the rest of us. She doesn't view them as stand-alone items, but rather as part of a larger, interdependent system, or what Deming would call a "systems view." Starting with this systems view, Jenkins could pull out another lens, which focuses on a certain aspect of the system. This lens might, for example, analyze the underlying assumptions that created the system and policies in the first place. Under this micro-lens, her clients might realize, for example, that their attendance policy is based on the outdated assumption that people can't be trusted, in direct conflict with one of the company's core values—trust.

After this examination, Jenkins helps her clients revise their assumptions to accurately reflect their core beliefs. These new assumptions then become the starting point for creatively redesigning HR policies and management practices. At the end of the engagement, a new system emerges in complete alignment with the company's values and goals.

Stanton, a mechanical engineer by training, looks at human resource systems with the troubleshooting orientation of an engineer. One of his engineering lenses, Failure Mode Effects Analysis (FMEA), allows him to see the hidden, unintended consequences that others often miss. In the world of automobile manufacturing where Stanton cut his teeth, failure to predict and avoid the unintended consequences of faulty system design can result in costly recalls, or worse, death. Given his background, Stanton can't help but see all systems through the FMEA strategic lens.

But in the world of human resources, where the negative consequences of system defects are less measurable and more insidious, Failure Mode Effects Analysis (FMEA) is not a common lens through which to view systems design. For example, an HR team may decide to add Pay for Performance to their incentive system and see only positive outcomes. Stanton sees the good, but the engineer in him can't help but think through the chain of consequences and all the bad places they could lead. He sees how, if not constructed properly, Pay for Performance could actually discourage more people than it motivates. Seeing this, Stanton, Jenkins, and the client team create a modified version of Pay for Performance that delivers all the good aspects while avoiding the unintended consequences. That's creativity. And it was inspired by looking at the problem through a different strategic lens than Jenkins's or the client team's.

When Jenkins and Stanton bring lenses from two different fields into a new one, they're replicating what Frans Johansson refers to in his book *The Medici Effect: Breakthrough Insights at the Intersection of Ideas, Concepts and Cultures*. The secret to unleashing a renaissance of thought is the same now as it was when we were emerging from the Dark Ages—bring in talented thinkers from different disciplines to look at the problems of the day through their various sets of lenses.

You can tap into this same effect by seeking out frameworks and principles from outside of your profession and reapplying them within it (for example, researching the principles of storytelling to make yourself a better teacher). Or bring in experts from outside your profession to help you think about your problem. If you do the latter, don't let the experts escape without teaching you a few of the lenses they employ. Remember, the more lenses you own, the more you can look through, and the more different ideas you'll see. In this case, greed is good. This is no time for austerity!

As you look through these lenses, remember to think of them as what-if questions. If we look at HR challenges through the lens of systems thinking as Jenkins does, we're simply asking, "What if we looked at this problem from a quality-based systems orientation? What ideas might we see?" By thinking of your different lenses as "what ifs," you give yourself the freedom to look through more of them because you drop the expectation that any one lens will provide the entire answer, or even part of the answer. Any lens holds the potential to lead you to a winning idea, part of a winning idea, or nowhere. But you'll never know until you try it on.

Finally, consider this: whether you know it or not, you and your team solve every problem with the same lenses. Unless you consciously seek out alternative ways of viewing your problem, you limit your creativity in much the same way as when you fixate on one right question.

Sharing the wealth across an organization, division, functional area, or team

Based on what they've read and remembered, everyone carries a unique collection of strategic lenses around in their head. The problem is that there is no sharing of these strategic nuggets or frameworks. It's as if each of us has our own set of amazing strategic x-ray glasses that allows us to see new ideas, but none of us think to offer our glasses to others—only I can see the ideas that come from my frameworks. As Sun Tzu states in the chapter-opening quote, we can see the tactics and the ideas, but we never see the strategic thought behind it. And if, as business author Michael Porters contends in the other quote, great CEOs are the ones who teach strategy, then obviously the sharing of these strategies is critical for our creativity and the success of our organizations. But is that the best use of a CEO's time? Is there a better way to transfer the knowledge from your best strategists to the rest of the company?

What if you gathered their strategic ways of looking at things, wrote them down (with necessary explanation), and placed them in a central location. This way, everyone can look through these lenses to solve problems creatively (and strategically). Think of it as a TRIZ for seeing strategic options. Current technology enables us to share strategic lenses so everyone can access them, rather than have them scattered about in random brains and home bookshelves. The strategic lenses in your most strategic employees' heads represent a highly valuable corporate asset. It only makes sense to aggregate these in one place so they can be taught and shared.

Here's a quick way to make this happen. Put someone in charge of the process, ideally someone who's strategic, who regularly uses knowledge of strategy to generate new options, and who's secure enough in his or her position and beliefs to share their competitive advantage with the rest of the team. That person should then:

1. Interview top strategists in the company and gather all the strategic lenses relevant to your organization or functional area. These will include unique ways your top thinkers frame problems and the principles or frameworks they've borrowed from key books.

2. Figure out a format to convey each lens or framework. Books like *The Profit Zone* already have succinct summaries you can use. The true test of your summarizing format is whether someone unfamiliar with a particular strategic principle can quickly grasp it and reapply it to their problem as a "what if."

3. Think about and gather lenses from outside your field that might have relevance to yours. What is your field or business similar to? What are you trying to accomplish, and who's attempting to accomplish the same? Thinking in terms of analogy will lead you to new fields, industries, or subject areas, and the unique sets of lenses they regularly use.

4. Create a place to store all your lenses and a time to introduce them to others.

Building a central bank of strategic lenses serves not only as a rich idea-generating tool, but in the process your people will become more like the strategic-creative folks I described in the beginning of the chapter.

To build your collection over time, continue to analyze the strategic successes around you. Nearly every highly successful company, organization, or individual did something strategically smart to become successful in the first place. Think about what they did and why it worked, then succinctly capture it as a strategic principle or framework. Once you do, you'll have created a new strategic lens you can add to the list and refer to in the future for new ideas.

Questions Beyond "What If"

I've chosen the what-if format because it represents one very good, time-proven way to ask stimulating questions. Some classics never go out of style, and the what-if question is one of them. Furthermore, using a questioning method with a common format gives all employees—and all people, for that matter—a common creative language. When stuck, someone can say, "Let's ask some what-if questions," and you'll all know what that means and why you're doing it. When someone starts a question with "what if," it should say to everyone in your organization, "I'm asking this question to help stimulate ideas, so don't judge the question or judge me, just back off and tell me what you see!"

As valuable as what-if questions are to creativity, they aren't the only kinds of questions you can ask. Some provocative questions won't start with "what if," and simply wouldn't work with that structure. The sheer number of possible questions and question types renders it impossible to represent them all here. Trust me. I attempted to collect and categorize all manner of idea-provoking questions for this book, and two years later landed on the conclusion that it was best to keep it simple and just focus on "what if." The purpose of the book is not to overwhelm you, but rather to make the goal of becoming more creative achievable.

Because there are a mind-boggling number of questions you could ask, don't fall into the opposite of the "One Right Question" trap, the "Have I Asked Every Question?" paranoia. You'll never ask every question. You'll always leave good questions undiscovered, unasked. Using the STAB and thinking of strategic lenses as "what ifs" will help you come up with more questions, but not every question. And that's okay. Even one extra question is already twice as good as what you had.

Here's another way to think about it. If you wanted to increase your leg strength, there are hundreds of exercises you could do. Yet if one exercise, lunges, could get you eighty percent of the way there, is it better to do lunges or better to do nothing and worry about all the exercises you're not doing? Asking "what if" is that one exercise.

So, forget all the things you could do and keep it simple. Just establishing the one habit of thinking "what if" more often will make you more creative.

• • •

In the final part of the book, I've put everything you've learned into a handy playbook you can use over and over. I've also assembled all the key terms into a kind of creativity glossary. This gives you and the people you work with a common language, so you're all using the same words, with the same meanings, and the same expectations. Only by sharing a common language and a common process will you move forward in your quest to become more creative as a unit.

You're almost there!

The Old Creativity	The New Creativity
Being strategic isn't being creative.	Being strategic is a way of being creative.
How your best strategists think remains invisible to others.	How your best strategists think is captured and shared with others.

Part Three

Planning

for

Success

Shared Process and Language

Think of this book three ways:

First, as a personal guidebook that teaches you two simple disciplines to become a more creative person.

Second, as a common playbook so your entire company can follow a similar process when it comes to pursuing creativity.

Finally, as a type of creativity glossary that will give you and the people you work with a common language, so you're all using the same words, with the same meanings, and the same expectations in your pursuit.

A shared process and shared language will move you forward in your quest to become more creative as a unit. Part Three will make that goal a reality.

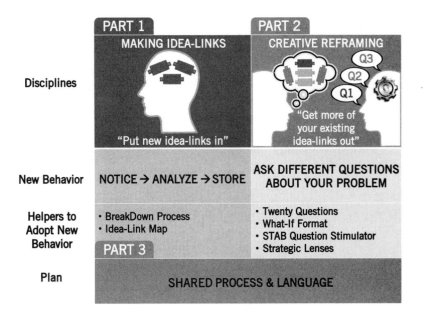

11

A Shared Process

Reduce your plan to writing. The moment you complete this, you will have definitely given concrete form to the intangible desire.

—NAPOLEON HILL, AMERICAN AUTHOR

*Everyone has a plan
'til they get punched in the mouth.*

—MIKE TYSON, AMERICAN PUGILIST

In a strange and wonderful coincidence, a little brown box landed on my porch as I started this chapter. Inside was something called P90X, a wildly successful "extreme" home exercise program my seventeen-year-old son asked me to order, presumably for us to do together.

If you're not familiar with P90X, here's all you need to know about why they've succeeded. First, P90X focused on an insight that intuitively, we already knew: Muscles get bored with the same workout, so you have to continually change what you're doing to maintain growth and avoid the dreaded plateau. Then, the P90X folks flexed their marketing muscle and in a stroke of pure genius, named their unique solution something cool and memorable: muscle confusion.

Inside the box, thirteen different DVDs work together to confound, stupefy, and thoroughly confuse your muscles. As I read DVD titles like *Ab Ripper X*, I can't help but think my muscles won't get confused so much as they'll just get angry. Really, really angry. But, I have to applaud P90X; taking a known consumer insight (muscles get bored) then giving their solution a unique and memorable name (like muscle confusion) is a good idea and a great new-product-success-factor idea-link to file away.

The other part of P90X's success lies in the detailed plan they provide. To truly confuse your muscles, you must follow—exactly—their schedule for confusing yourself. In a weird twist, they've actually made confusion simple. Read their material and there's no question what's needed to get started or what schedule to follow or how long to follow it. The message is simple—follow this for ninety days and you'll parade around in a beach body. It's all about following the plan. Here's why plans matter.

Researchers have found that keeping a resolution has little to do with willpower, even though lack of willpower is the most commonly cited reason for failing to make positive changes. We think it's about willpower, but it's really about something else. And to understand why, you need to understand the brain.[60] The place in your brain where willpower

resides—the prefrontal cortex—can easily become over-
whelmed by other demands in your life. It's not that your
will went away—you still want to get in shape or lose
weight—it's just that other thoughts and mental demands
bullied willpower out of the place in the brain where you
held it.

That's why you go to business seminars convinced
you'll be a changed person at work, only to have the stresses
of meeting tight deadlines and juggling multiple projects
overwhelm your prefrontal cortex and shove your resolve
back in your brain. In short time, you return to being the
same person you were, doing
the same things you did before
the seminar, while the seminar
leader flies to his next city with
a wad of cash, some of it yours.

Failure to plan for success,
not lack of willpower, is the
most common reason
a resolution fails

Failure to plan for success,
not lack of willpower, is the most common reason a resolution fails, be it a New Year's resolution, or a resolution
to become more creative. If you want to get in shape but
haven't purchased workout clothes, or entered your workout
dates on your calendar, or committed to meeting with a
personal trainer, or glued some crazy P90X schedule on
your basement wall, you'll simply return to your old habits
once you get busy with life. Having a plan and scheduling
it takes your resolve from your prefrontal cortex and plants
it firmly into your life. Think of resolutions and willpower
as lightweight wimps, easily jostled out of place. Plans and
schedules, on the other hand, hold their place in your life—
they've got roots and staying power.

So don't think about converting your resolution to
become more creative into action. Think through how to

translate your resolution to become more creative into a plan. It's the plan, written down, that supports follow-through on your resolution, even when your initial resolve gets punched in the mouth by the rest of your work life.

Without a written plan, you'll eventually default to the path of least resistance—what you've always done, the way you've always done it. You'll always be too busy; always have too much to do. A plan in your head isn't really a plan, it's an intention. You need a plan.

So first, before we make the plan, what have you resolved after reading this far? I hope by now I've made a case that organizations with bigger storehouses of idea-links and a greater willingness to ask more questions will build and draw more creativity from their people. I further hope you'll make your own resolution to hunt and gather new idea-links. And that you'll resolve to begin asking more and more revealing questions to draw them out of yourself and others.

Now about that plan . . .

If you're a natural planner and planning is your greatest pleasure, I don't want to steal your fun. Go ahead and outline your own approach, or meet with your team to decide how you want to approach the planning process.

If you want a plan to work from, P90X-style, I've included (on the following page) a description of a process I've used with my client companies. You won't get a beach body, but you will get creatively ripped. Like any workout, you can decide to do it alone, or as a group or team. I've written the plan assuming you'll do this as a team. If that's not the case, you should find it easy to adapt it for individual use. Whatever you choose—my plan, your plan, or a hybrid plan—you need to get your plan written down. At the end of this section is a template for you to fill in to get the process started.

Getting Creatively Ripped in a Subject Area

Step 1   Decide how you'll store your idea-links.

Step 2   Determine what you want to get creative about.

Step 3   Teach people what idea-links are and how to create them.

Step 4   Pick one creative focus area and set a goal.

Step 5   Gather idea-links for your focus area (notice/find, analyze, store).

Step 6   Review idea-links as a group and gather ideas.

Step 7   Pick another area. Repeat steps 1–6.

Step 8   Schedule ongoing idea-linking.

Step 1: Decide how you'll store your idea-links.

Before you begin generating idea-links and other creative assets, create a place to store them (remember a place for everything, everything in its place). As an individual, you can commit your idea-links to memory, though you'll do much better if you store them in a place where they won't get lost and you can regularly revisit them. If you're just doing this for yourself, that might mean creating an Excel spreadsheet or a hanging file that's always accessible, a la Jack Gust. The advantage of a spreadsheet is you can code your idea-links by type, and then sort and print them as needed. The advantage of a physical file is the ability to save the articles, ads, or reports from where the idea-link originated. You also need to think through how you'll catch the idea-links you come across randomly throughout your day. I carry index cards with me to capture them, one per card, and then stick them in a file. I'm not much of a spreadsheet guy, and I don't work at a corporation, so this is as far as I go unless I need them for a creative session (then I turn them into laminated cards). Some people send themselves emails from their smart phone. You'll simply have to figure out what you'll use to record your idea-links—a small notebook, your cell phone, or index cards—and where you're going to put them. But you do have to figure something out if you want a system that's more reliable than just memory and recall.

This isn't to say that memory isn't an option. What memory loses in recall, it gains in ease of use. Using just your memory requires the least amount of work and pre-planning. You're simply saying to yourself, "I'm going to try to make idea-links more often and attempt to take mental note of them when I do. I'll remember what I remember." Each storage method comes with trade-offs.

If you're part of a team, functional area, or organization, you need to think beyond your own self-interest and decide what works best for the entire team. Relying on memory isn't enough. The only way for everyone to benefit from each other's idea-links is to put them in place where they can be easily aggregated and accessed by anyone, anytime. This probably means some type of virtual storehouse. You could check with your internal IT people and tell them you want to create an internal website where you can add information, code it, then retrieve it using the codes. (More about coding in Step 2.)

If you don't have an internal person, or if this sounds like too much work, check TheNewCreativity.com. I'm working on my own web-based program and will post it there when it's completed.

Step 2: Determine what you want to get creative about.

Before you go about gathering idea-links, find subject areas where you, your team, your functional area, or your company wants to expand creativity. That will help you determine which sort codes or labels to create. If cost savings ideas are important, then make a code or a tab labeled "cost-saving idea-links." This then becomes your own, ever-expanding idea-link data bank for cost-saving creativity. Your list will be to cost savings what TRIZ is to engineering, except yours will continue to grow.

Gather your team and ask them what they think they need to become more creative about. In most cases, I've found that groups agree on areas quickly, albeit with some variation in what they call the areas or how broadly they define them. You needn't get this step perfect. Just get the labels down and entered into the document or website as place-holders if you're doing it electronically, or create different files if you're going old-school. You can always change things later, renaming areas, or collapsing or dividing them.

Step 3: Teach people what idea-links are and how to create them.

One of the key reasons the concept of idea-links works is because it gives a common language to creativity's raw material. If you're doing this as a team or company, you must all have the same understanding to succeed. With a common understanding in place, you can look for and gather the right things, and avoid the wrong things—for example, gathering idea-links (the right things), and not facts (the wrong things).

If you were asking your team to collect clams on the beach but you couldn't describe a clam and how it differs from the other items on the beach, your team would return with a bucket full of rocks, cigarette butts, tar balls, and the occasional clam. Reread the early chapters until you're fully satisfied you can explain idea-links and how you make them. Understanding what an idea-link is and isn't will keep the tar balls and cigarette butts out of your communal idea-link bucket.

Step 4: Pick one creative focus area and set a goal.

Once you have your areas outlined and your people trained, I recommend you pick just one area to start. Get the entire team focused on cost savings, for example, and build your bank of cost-saving idea-links by looking inside and outside the company and your current category or industry. Give the team a set period of time, say one month. And give them a goal—perhaps fifty idea-links.

Step 5: Gather idea-links for your focus area.

Remember to follow the three steps of making idea-links. *Notice* (or find) examples that are interesting, *analyze* what makes them work or succeed, *store* a succinct explanation. On the "find" side, think about where you'll actively look for idea-links related to your subject area. On the "notice" side, think about the types of things you want to put on your radar screen. If this is confusing, look at the sample template later in the chapter as an example.

Step 6: Review idea-links as a group and gather ideas.

Once you have fifty idea-links (or whatever your goal is), have each group member review the entire pool of idea-links and write down new ideas for ways your company can cut costs (to continue the cost-saving example). Then, plan a session where people share the ideas they've generated and tell the story of the idea-link that inspired it. This will help reinforce the notion that idea-links birth ideas.

A session like this might take two or three hours; the more idea-links, the longer the meeting (and the more ideas you'll harvest). Make sure to put it on the calendar before the idea-link gathering begins so your team knows they have a deadline, and that they're expected to produce. Future dates solidify plans and force people to act.

The other option is to not do individual work in advance, but instead hold a session where everybody reviews the idea-links at once, generating ideas during the session. With the right website functionality, you can also do this virtually by allowing group members to review idea-links, then enter ideas into the website. Each virtual attendee can then use both idea-links and new ideas as creative stimulus.

Step 7: Pick another area (repeat 1–6).

Once you've completed one area, move on to the next critical area. After you've gone through all the areas important to you, eventually everyone will get a feel for the kinds of idea-links that appear in each area and instinctively know what to be alert for going forward. That way, your whole group can add idea-links to the database as they're discovered, in an organic rather than forced fashion.

Step 8: Schedule ongoing idea-linking.

Once you reach this point, you have an established base of idea-links that grows on its own. You should still, however, arrange for specific events—"idea-link drives"—to renew the communal bank. You might want to add idea-links to an existing area, or feed a new area where you identify a need to get creative. For example, perhaps you've struggled to come up with creative ways to generate prelaunch buzz for your new products. Create a new category called "publicity or buzz-creation idea-links" and get to work. Or you may simply want to bolster an existing area by turning loose a new group of people with fresh eyes to see what new idea-links they unearth.

Plan for specific collection times by giving people a topic area, a clear time frame, and a collection goal, but also allow for random contributions to any topic area at any time once the areas are set up and initially populated.

Putting Your Plan in Writing

Whether you plan to go through the entire process as a team, or just decide to become more creative on your own, it helps to commit your plan to writing. On the following page is a sample planning template for someone in the package design business (you can download a blank one from the website). Using a template like this on your own provides focus and direction; using it as a team puts you all on the same page and allows you to divvy up tasks.

Sample Plan

How I/we will store idea-links:

Website, accessed by all our package designers

What I/we need to become more creative about (list up to three areas):

1) *Package design solutions*
2) *Cost-saving opportunities*
3) *Selling our ideas to marketing*

First focus area (pick one from the list of three above):

Package design solutions

Goal—number of idea-links to collect:

30 (6 per team member)

Date, time, and location to review idea-links:

March 30th, 2pm to 5pm, Room 222

Possible places to look for idea-links related to this area (finding and analyzing stuff that already exists):

1) *Food products that have solved portability issues via packaging innovation*
2) *New packages that were revolutionary when introduced*
3) *Package design winners over the last 10 years (check various sources)*

Things I should put on my radar screen for this area (noticing and analyzing new stuff):

1) *Any innovative packages we see in our industry*
2) *Innovative package designs in other industries that solve a consumer problem*
3) *Any innovative approach to structural design (non-packaging) that improves an end user's experience (homes, cars, luggage, etc.)*

Getting Creative for a Specific Project or Problem

If you need to become more creative about a specific project, rather than become generally more creative in a subject area, you need to add a few steps. For one, it won't be as obvious where to look for idea-links. That's when you use the BreakDown Questions.

The other aspect that's different is the need to ask different questions or look at the problem through different strategic lenses. Subject areas are broad, but problems or projects are usually defined by a single objective or question (the "right" one). That specificity, while good for alignment, can often lock you into a certain kind of thinking that will limit your ideas. You break out of this trap by using creative reframing.

If you want a detailed, step-by-step process for a specific project, you can download a PDF at TheNewCreativity.com.

• • •

What both processes do is provide some structure to the goal of becoming more creative as a person, and especially as a team. You move from a bunch of people walking around blindly, all doing their own thing with their own language, continually having to recreate ideas from blank slates, to a disciplined team collecting, organizing, sharing, and accessing the same creative assets, using the same creative language.

We'll take care of the language part in the next chapter.

The Old Creativity	The New Creativity
Creativity can't be planned.	Improving your creativity must be planned.

12

A Shared Vocabulary

Diversity: the art of thinking independently together.
—MALCOLM FORBES, AMERICAN PUBLISHER

If chapter eleven is the new playbook for you or your company to become more creative, this chapter contains the key words you'll use as you execute the playbook. To succeed, you need both. You can diagram the perfect play in football or basketball, but if no one on the team understands words like pass, block, or fake, there's a good chance the play will disintegrate into chaos.

There are no new words in the glossary that follows— you've seen them all earlier in the book—so why bring them all together in one place, in its own chapter? Because no team, tribe, or troop can hope to accomplish anything significant without a shared vocabulary, and right now creativity doesn't have one. We all want more creativity, yet we've no idea how to talk about it. Telling your team they need to be more creative and then offering no further direction is like a coach telling his football team they need more touchdowns and then hoping they score. Even prehistoric hunters had grunts and hand signals as they pursued their goal. When it comes to pursuing creativity, we're an evolutionary step behind the Neanderthal.

Some of you might worry that a common vocabulary will hurt creativity. That it makes everyone the same. On the contrary, the intrinsic value found in diversity of thought can only be captured when, as Forbes puts it, you think independently *together.* And the only way to think together is to speak the same language and work from the same glossary.

Use the terms presented here and add new ones as you create them. Like most of the book, I'm giving you a starting point to work from. If you do generate new terms, processes, or procedures, write them down and define them in a format similar to what's presented below. That will ensure your shared vocabulary doesn't take on conflicting meanings, which is worse than having no vocabulary in the first place.

You use a shared language in every other important endeavor in your organization. Creativity deserves no less.

Glossary of Creativity Terms and Phrases

BreakDown Process/Questions: A process used when trying to solve a problem or to inject more creativity into a project. The BreakDown Process will lead you to the places where you're likely to find new idea-links. It's based upon two simple questions:

> BreakDown Question 1: What do I want to accomplish and who has already accomplished the same thing?

> BreakDown Question 2: What are the barriers to solving my problem and who else has dealt with similar barriers?

Think of the BreakDown Process as a divining rod to find analogies.

cataloging: The process of recording idea-links and strategic lenses, then adding them to a permanent location where they can be stored and accessed.

creative assets: Any of the idea-links, questions, or strategic lenses generated by individuals or teams that have been cataloged so they can be easily accessed and used repeatedly to build creativity and generate ideas.

creative reframing: The process of taking an existing question or problem statement and restating it in different ways, or asking different questions, for the purpose of seeing new ideas. The focus of this process is on asking new, potentially revealing questions, not on finding the "right" one.

idea-link: A succinct insight or realization about why or how something works or succeeds that is stored into memory. Idea-links are the product of curiosity-driven analysis.

Idea-Link Map: A comprehensive, visual representation of the BreakDown Process. A completed map shows the areas you looked toward for inspiration, the idea-links you extracted, and the ideas you generated.

idea-linking: The process of analyzing examples in order to extract idea-links.

judge-hole: Any individual who ruins an interesting story or idea with his or her own judgment, thereby killing curiosity in its tracks before anything valuable (such as an idea-link) might get extracted.

STAB/taking a STAB: A SWOT-like tool used to help individuals or teams stimulate new questions. Acronym for:

> **S**ix circumstances (who, what, where, when, why, and how)
>
> **T**raits
>
> **A**ssumptions
>
> **B**arriers

strategic lens/strategic frameworks: Any strategic summation that can be used to help you generate ideas by thinking of them as what-if questions. Typically, these come from business books, though may be self-generated by analyzing the strategic success of others.

twenty questions: The process of taking your original question and forcing yourself to ask twenty new questions, and with little or no self-censorship.

"what ifs": A preferred form of questioning that reduces the chances of sounding foolish and increases the chance of spurring the imagination.

The Old Creativity	The New Creativity
Creativity is a mystery with no common language.	Creativity requires a common language.

13

Final Words of Encouragement

Genius is finding the invisible link between things.
—Vladimir Nabokov, Russian novelist

We'll probably never know *exactly* how creativity works. Because it occurs in the brain, involving circuitry we didn't build and processes we can't see, we make our best guesses about what's going on in there. It's kind of like knowing exactly how the sun works—we can make educated guesses, but none of us were there to see how it was formed, and we can't see inside it. So we do our best to understand, based on the evidence around us. In truth, no one will ever completely crack the creative code, only important parts of it.

In 2007, I first proposed the concept of idea-links as creativity's "invisible link" and introduced the notion that creative people are actually highly analytical. Rather than rushing to write this book, I've been continually gathering evidence to support my theory, while at the same time, encouraging others to shoot it down.

Certainly, someone could make the case that there is more to creativity than just idea-link making and creative reframing. I have to agree, there is, but that doesn't mean that idea-link making and creative reframing aren't tremendously important contributors to creative ability. In addition, the other factors that might determine individual creativity are largely out of your control. Idea-link making and creative reframing, on the other hand, are firmly in your control to adopt or ignore.

If you remain a skeptic, here's the best evidence I can give you. I have an idea company, and aha moments occur around me by the hundreds every month. If they didn't, my business would be in trouble. I'm in the habit of asking my clients, at the moment they hatch an idea, before they have time to over-think things, or to retrofit a different story, how they got that idea. I find out what series of connections transpired and where the connecting material came from.

I find that nearly every time a great idea occurs, it's because the creator has pulled some thought from his or her past and connected it to the current problem. When asked where the thought came from, he or she usually shares a story of some experience or curiosity-driven analysis that produced the connecting thought. This thought had been stored away in memory for no particular reason. These thoughts now have a name. I call them idea-links.

In my ideation sessions, I also regularly observe how posing a new question suddenly triggers a roomful of ideas almost instantaneously, whereas prior to the question, the group remained certain that all possible ideas were already on the table. It's obvious that asking lots of questions unlocks idea-links that already exist in our brains.

My biggest worry through this process was how highly creative people would perceive my idea-link theory. To my surprise, creative people became its biggest fans because the concept of idea-links helps them finally explain to others why they think and behave the way they do. Nearly all the highly creative folks who attend my workshops confide in me afterward that indeed, this is what they do (make idea-links and ask questions), but until now, they were never conscious of what they were doing, didn't have a name for it, or assumed that everybody was doing the same thing. They leave pleased that their coworkers (and spouses) can now appreciate their idiosyncrasies as simply part of what makes them creative people. And they are pleased that others now better understand how their behavior ultimately creates value for the organization. After talking to creative people, I remain convinced that creating idea-links is what creative people do and that they have more idea-links than the general population because of their high level of curiosity.

But perhaps most important to me is the response from those who came to my sessions thinking they weren't very creative and could never become more creative—the ones who had given up. I hope I've proven to you that you already are creative in some way, or in some area of life, and that you have the capacity to become even more creative. At the end of one workshop, someone told me, "If that's what it takes to be more creative, I can do that. This makes sense. This actually gives me hope."

I hope this book gives you hope as well.

You won't have to change your hairstyle, drive a new way to work each day, or move your watch from one wrist to the other to become more creative. What I've told you works. I've simply taken what has always been happening at an unconscious level, brought it to a conscious level, and labeled it so you can do it on your own and have a common vocabulary to talk about it with others. I've simply taken some of the mystery out of creativity, and in doing so, given us all a chance to produce more of it.

I asked you to give me a chance to show you that you can become more creative without having to wear a wacky hat or rainbow wig to get there. Thank you for giving me that chance. I hope the next time you do something silly, you're doing it because you feel like it, not because someone is trying to mandate your fun. It's much better that way.

• • •

I welcome your comments and ideas. You can reach me a number of ways:

▶ E-mail me at **Jim@idea-link.com**

▶ Connect with me on **LinkedIn**

▶ Visit **TheNewCreativity.com**, say hello, and sign up to receive free idea-links

The Old Creativity

Become more creative by sorting through hundreds of creative exercises, tips, and techniques.

The New Creativity

Become more creative by practicing two simple disciplines.

Recommended Reading and Resources

Selected Reading List for Strategic Lenses

Marketing Warfare by Al Reis and Jack Trout

All books by Reis and Trout brim with strategy idea-links because the authors have a certain genius for taking what works and distilling it down to usable nuggets. The twentieth-anniversary edition features updated stories in addition to its original stories. Working in marketing and not knowing these principles is like working in chemistry without knowing solubility rules: something will blow up in your face. Memorize the rules of each kind of warfare and make sure you understand the principle they represent. These principles make great what-if questions you can use over and over, especially when faced with a competitive situation.

The 22 Immutable Laws of Marketing: Violate Them at Your Own Risk! by Al Reis and Jack Trout

Here, the genius of Reis and Trout is distilled down to twenty-two laws. Take a law, like "Law of the Opposite," and turn it into a question: "What if we positioned our product in a way that's opposite of the market leader? What would that look like?" Answer: It may not lead you to the right idea, but it will lead you to a new idea. That's the intent.

Made to Stick: Why Some Ideas Survive and Others Die by Dan Heath and Chip Heath

Made to Stick is a beautifully written book about how to better communicate your idea so it "sticks" in people's heads. If you work in communications, sales, marketing, or advertising, this book is a must-remember. Not a must-read, but a must-remember book. That means reading it and leaving with the Heath brothers' SUCCES mnemonic framework firmly planted in your head so you can use it in the future. Each letter in the acronym can be turned into a what-if question that will help you generate creative ways to make your idea stickier.

The Profit Zone: How Strategic Business Design Will Lead You to Tomorrow's Profits by Adrian J. Slywotzky and David J. Morrison, with Bob Andelman

If you work in finance or new product innovation, then you must have this book, which I briefly mentioned in chapter six. In *The Profit Zone*, the authors analyzed hundreds of businesses and reduced them to twenty or so business models. Think of it as the TRIZ of business models. If you need to solve a problem and your current business model doesn't work, it's a great source of creative inspiration. You can simply look at each business model and say, "What if we used this business model, what ideas might we see?"

The Innovator's Solution: Creating and Sustaining Successful Growth by Clayton M. Christensen & Michael E. Raynor

While you won't get as many lenses here, the two "disruption" lenses the authors describe will help you see new ways to generate business opportunities, particularly if you're entering an existing industry or category. Looking through these two lenses will help you see ideas and strategies you might otherwise miss. If you're the incumbent in an industry, looking at your own industry through these same lenses will show you how you might be attacked by a new entrant. From there, it's up to you to decide your course of action.

Blue Ocean Strategy: How to Create Uncontested Market Space and Make Competition Irrelevant
by W. Chan Kim and Renée Mauborgne

Blue Ocean Strategy contains a hefty collection of strategic lenses, though not as cleanly arranged as *Marketing Warfare* or *The 22 Immutable Laws*. Some lenses are called "actions" (The Four Actions) whereas others are labeled "paths" (Six Paths to Reconstruct Market Boundaries). Regardless of the moniker, if you take the time to look through each one as a "what if," you'll end up with new ideas.

Selected Reading List for Creative Exercise Books

Creative exercise books hold a very important place in the world of ideation, but you have to know their limitations. They'll help you come up with ideas. But, they generally won't make you any more creative after you use them than a joke book would make you a funnier person after reading a joke (even though telling the joke creates laughs). That's why I've made the important distinction between this book, which is about making you steadily more creative over time, and exercise books, which help you create an idea at this moment (if you happen to use the right exercise).

If you're planning an ideation or need some good exercises, there are lots of books to choose from. I recommend these two.

Serious Creativity: Using the Power of Lateral Thinking to Create New Ideas by Edwin de Bono

De Bono is the father of what I refer to as "intentional creativity." His concept of lateral thinking helps explain why certain exercises, like the random word exercise, or challenging assumptions, will create new ideas. You'll see that he and I have some differences in how we explain *why* these exercises generate ideas, but I greatly respect his work and intellect nonetheless. *Serious Creativity*, though now over twenty years old, remains a worthwhile summation of de Bono's many books. It will offer you an alternative to my way of thinking about creativity.

Brain Boosters for Business Advantage: Ticklers, Grab Bags, Blue Skies, and Other Bionic Ideas by Arthur B. VanGundy

Brain Boosters is by far the best creative exercise reference book. Dr. VanGundy, a professor at the University of Oklahoma, compiled a wide variety of proven exercises from his own ideation work and those of select others, such as Doug Hall. What makes this book especially valuable is how VanGundy teaches you to perform each exercise in a step-by-step fashion. It also includes a handy index to help locate exercises that work especially well with certain types of challenges (new products, strategic problems, human resource issues, etc.). If you're going to do creative exercises, or need to plan an ideation, this is a good book to own.

Acknowledgements

Idea-Links took me five years to write. Five years seems like a long time, until I realized that I had actually worked on this book my entire life. I've always had a deep fascination with ideas—how they happen, how to get more of them, and why some people generate them more easily than others. You might say I'm addicted to ideas, but in a good way.

Steve Jobs reflected in his famous "Stay Hungry, Stay Foolish" commencement address at Stanford that you can never connect the dots of your career looking forward, you can only connect them looking back. In hindsight, this book about creativity was destined to happen. I see that now. I can also see that my most important dots weren't events or places, but people. I owe this book to the friends, family, mentors, clients, coworkers, and coconspirators who influenced, shaped, contributed, challenged, cajoled, and guided me along the way. Among them:

My former bosses and mentors at General Mills who were kind enough to encourage my strengths, and even kinder to point out and help me address my weaknesses. I'm especially grateful to Carol Gullstad, Christi Strauss, Ian

Friendly, and Jeff Rotsch. Jeff was particularly proficient at the "pointing out my weaknesses" part.

I am grateful to the many clients and collaborators who have sustained me over the years, more than just monetarily. I hope to eventually thank you all, but must first acknowledge Steve Audette, Sharon Remien, and Anna Stoesz of General Mills, who called me in 2007 to deliver the speech that would become this book, and Sandra Clifford, Spike Carlsen, Gregg Hietpas, Tim Moynihan, George Abide, Fran Johns, Mark Addicks, and Joe Ens, who encouraged me to keep it going. I'm fortunate to have a wealth of innovative companies like General Mills in my backyard, filled with supportive folks who helped with the book, or who gave me confidence that people would actually read it. Among them were 3Mers past and present, Jean Enloe, Debbie Barron, Jean Chaput, Bonnie Nichol, Jolene Conard, Tom Herbrand, Steve Henry, Timm Hammond, Gretchen Hauble, Glenn Carter, Anne Greer, Bob Holler, Mike Smith, Andy Ouderkirk, Curt Larson, Wayne Lindholm, Kim Johnson, Dave Braun, and Art Fry. Also, John Wright, Dana Lonn, and the king of e-mail trash-talk, Jack Gust at Toro; Arya Badiyan and Dagmara Wrzecionkowska at Nestlé; Pam Moret at Thrivent; and Bob Wolf at Andersen Windows. At Land O' Lakes, Barry Wolfish, the "Michelles" (Freedman and Kopp), Luis Moreno, and Jodi Moore (who pushed me to drop my modesty and call my "things" idea-links even though it was also my company name and partly my last name—sometimes the most obvious answer is right in front of you).

All those who helped with the writing and research in big and little ways, including Adam Swenson, Lindsay Berger, Brian Graff, Dr. Thom Davis, George Abide, Jack

Hartmann, Matt Smith, Hans Birkholz, John Link, Rusty Fischer, Laurie Harper, Mary Jenkins, and Peter Horst. Sometimes, even the smallest suggestion opened up an entirely new area of exploration. Developmental editor Leslie Stephan of Austin, TX, who was kind enough to work with a first-time author; without her expert guidance, I would have surely lost my way. Copy editor Susan Foster, who added polish and kept me in good humor. Dara Beevas of indie publisher Beaver's Pond Press for helping me navigate the world of publishing, and Glenn Fuller, Mary Martin, and Jay Monroe, for the design work, which brought my thoughts to life. A special thanks to editors extraordinaire Lily Coyle and Wendy Weckwerth. If you found the book enjoyable to read, these two talented professionals are the reasons why.

And finally, thanks to everyone who approached me after my training seminars and speeches with encouraging words or ideas to make the content better. I did my best to write down your names, but my place-for-everything organizing system sometimes lets me down.

Some day, when you look back on your life's dot-connected journey, you'll probably notice one dot in particular that stands out. Without that dot, your series of connections probably wouldn't have brought you to where you are now. Of all the dots, it's the one that made the biggest difference.

Mine is Janet Goodwin, who became my through-richer-or-poorer dot twenty-some years ago, and now goes by Janet Link. Anyone who takes chances in life—pursuing your MBA at night for six years, leaving a promising career to start your own company at the age of thirty-three, taking five years to write a book—needs someone like Janet, either as a friend, a spouse, or a mentor. They're the ones who tell you to go for it, and then continue to tell you to go for it, even when you come home grumpy after a bad day of going for it. They're the ones who believe in you more than you believe in yourself. They're the ones who provide the encouraging push, and occasional shove, that turns dreams into reality.

If you're lucky enough to find a Janet in your life, hang on, because you'll end up going someplace wonderful. Just keep your hands off mine!

• • •

And special thanks to my mom, who told me I could be anything I wanted. I was listening.

Endnotes

1   Po Bronson and Ashley Merryman, "The Creativity Crisis," *Newsweek*, July 19, 2010, 44–50.

2   Unless otherwise noted, the examples cited are from my work or consulting experience or from personal interviews. The titles and companies of the people I describe may have changed since I first worked or talked with them.

3   Paul Simon, "The Songwriting Process," *iTunes Originals– Paul Simon*, accessed November 5, 2011. (No longer available on iTunes.com.)

4   Marc Eliot, *Paul Simon: A Life* (Hoboken, NJ: John Wiley & Sons, 2010), 22.

5   Lewis Corner, "Lady Gaga: Creative Process is Like Vomiting," *Digital Spy*, April 20, 2011, http://www.digitalspy. com/music/news/a315568/ lady-gaga-creative-process-is- like-vomiting.html.

6   Rolling Stone Online, "Lady Gaga Declares Herself 'Librarian of Glam Culture.'" *US Weekly*, May 12, 2011, http://www.rollingstone.com/ music/news/lady-gaga-declares- herself-librarian-of-glam- culture-20110512.

7   Wikipedia, "Lady Gaga," http:// en.wikipedia.org/wiki/Lady_ Gaga, accessed June 1, 2011.

8   Rolling Stone Online, "Lady Gaga Declares Herself 'Librarian of Glam Culture.'"

9   Frans Johansson, *The Medici Effect: Breakthrough Insights at the Intersection of Ideas, Concepts, and Cultures* (Boston: Harvard Business Press, 2004).

10   Wikipedia, "Farmville," http://en.wikipedia.org/wiki/ FarmVille, accessed August 10, 2011.

11   Nicholas Lovell, "Six Secrets of Farmville," GamesBrief.com, September 4, 2009, http:// www.gamesbrief.com/2009/09/ six-secrets-of-farmvilles-success- and-33-million-people-agree/.

12   Bill Keveney, "*American Idol* Finale Ratings Soar," *USA Today*, May 26, 2011, http:// www.usatoday.com/life/ television/news/2011-05-26- american-idol-ratings-soar_n. htm.

13   Freemantle Media, "Idols," http://www.fremantlemedia. com/Production/Our_brands/ Idols.aspx, viewed June 15, 2011.

14   Deconstructing the *Idol* formula appears courtesy of Jon Gutierrez, the principal and cofounder of St. Croix Prep Academy, who uses it to demonstrate how they teach kids to make connections. I've simply built on it.

15 Joseph Campbell, *The Hero with a Thousand Faces* (1st edition, Bollingen Foundation, 1949. 2nd edition, Princeton University Press. 3rd edition, New World Library, 2008).

16 cpowers94 (poster). "History of Gatorade 2," YouTube, October 26, 2008, http://www.youtube.com/watch?v=lWrJ0fxDhmg.

17 Greg Schneider, "Toyota's Prius Proving to Be the Hotter Ride in Hybrids: Head-Turning Gas-Electric Outsells Honda's Staid Version," *Washington Post*, August 23, 2004, http://www.washingtonpost.com/wp-dyn/articles/A24832-2004Aug22.html.

18 Vicki Haddock, "Oh, so pious, Prius drivers/Smugness drifts over the warming Earth—is that a bad thing?" sfgate.com, July 15, 2007, http://articles.sfgate.com/2007-07-15/opinion/17252123_1_hybrid-owners-hybrid-version-south-park. See also Micheline Maynard, "Say 'Hybrid' and Many People will Hear 'Prius,'" *New York Times*, July 7, 2004, http://www.nytimes.com/2007/07/04/business/04hybrid.html.

19 Robin McDonald, "The mileage game. But is it safe to play all the time?" August 20, 2009, http://priuschat.com/forums/newbie-forum/67620-mileage-game-its-fun-but-safe-play-all-time.html, accessed May 24, 2011.

20 I'm not sure who originally coined the term *fellowship of the Prius*, but it's used frequently among Prius bloggers.

21 See Steve Martin's acceptance speech for the Mark Twain Comedy Prize from November 9, 2005, at http://www.youtube.com/watch?v=Jxw73V_0h2Q.

22 Steve Martin, *Born Standing Up: A Comic's Life* (New York: Scribner, 2007), 51.

23 Geoffrey Macnab, "Italian B-Movies: Tarantino's Inspiration," *Independent Online*, February 2, 2006, http://news.bbc.co.uk/2/hi/uk_news/magazine/3712013.stm.

24 Andrew Walker, "Faces of the Week," *BBC News Online*, last updated May 14, 2004, http://news.bbc.co.uk/2/hi/uk_news/magazine/3712013.stm.

25 Nicholas Dawidoff, "Paul Simon's Restless Journey," *Rolling Stone*, May 12, 2011, 63.

26 Michael Snell, Kim Baker, and Sunny Baker, *From Book Idea to Bestseller: What You Absolutely, Positively Must Know to Make Your Book a Success* (Roseville, CA: Prima Lifestyles, 1997), 35.

27 Laurence Gonzales, *Deep Survival: Who Lives, Who Dies, and Why* (New York: W.W. Norton, 2004), 79–80. The study has since spawned a book, *The Invisible Gorilla: How Our Intuitions Deceive Us*, by the study's originators, Christopher Chabris and Daniel Simons (New York: Crown, 2010).

28 Megan Lane, "What Asperger's Syndrome has done for us," *BBC News Online Magazine,* June 2, 2004. http://news.bbc.co.uk/2/hi/3766697.stm.

29 Jaime Craig and Simon Baron-Cohen, "Creativity and imagination in autism and Asperger's Syndrome," *Journal of Autism and Developmental Disorders* no. 29 (1999): 319–326.

30 Simon Baron-Cohen, "The hyper-systemizing, assertive mating theory of autism," *Progress in Neuro-Pscychopharmacology & Biological Psychiatry* no. 30 (2006): 865–872.

31 Greene, Anthony J. "Making Connections," *Scientific American Mind,* July/August, 2010, 22–29.

32 Gonzales, 67.

33 Gonzales, 74.

34 John Terninko, *Step by Step QFD: Customer Driven Product Design* (Boca Raton, FL: CRC Press 1997), 179–192.

35 Leonid Lerner, "Genrich Altshuller: Father of TRIZ," excerpted from *Russian Magazine Ogonek,* 1991. http://www.aitriz.org/articles/altshuller.pdf.

36 Barry Feig, *Marketing Straight to the Heart: From New Product Development to Advertising—How Smart Companies Use the Power of Emotion to Win Loyal Customers* (New York: AMACOM, 1997).

37 Bruce Schreiner, "Colonel Sanders' Secret Recipe for KFC Leaves the Vault," *Houston Chronicle,* September 9, 2008, http://www.chron.com/disp/story.mpl/business/5991230.html.

38 Dee-Ann Durbin, "Build your own Corvette engine: GM's new offer will cost you $5,800," *St. Paul Pioneer Press,* July 13, 2010, 15a.

39 Adrian J. Slywotzky, David J. Morrison, and Bob Andelman, *The Profit Zone: How Strategic Business Design Will Lead You to Tomorrow's Profits* (New York: Crown, 2002).

40 Take Me Fishing™ National Campaign. ©RBFF, 2008, http://www.youtube.com/watch?v=U7cpTeAOb6M.

41 Daniel Gilbert, *Stumbling on Happiness* (New York: Knopf, 2006).

42 William J. Broad, "Subtle Analogies Found at the Core of Edison's Genius," *New York Times,* March 12, 1985, sec C.

43 Ibid.

44 See, for example, Will Weaver, *Sweet Land: New and Selected Stories* (St. Paul, MN: Borealis Books, 2006).

45 Michael Snell, Kim Baker, and Sunny Baker, *From Book Idea to Bestseller* (Rocklin, CA: Prima Lifestyles, 1997) 35.

46 Michael Lev, "Can UCS Navigate Oregon's Speed Trap?" ocregister.com, October 29, 2010, http://articles.

ocregister.com/2010-10-29/
sports/24819909_1_usc-coach-
lane-kiffin-oregon-ducks.

47 Michael Sokolove, "Speed-
Freak Football," *New York
Times Magazine*, December
2, 2010, http://www.
nytimes.com/2010/12/05/
magazine/05Football-t.
html?_r=1&pagewanted=1.

48 Sokolove, 5.

49 Sokolove, 5.

50 Rob Moseley, "UO Success a
Matter of Time," *The Register-
Guard*, October 27, 2010,
http://special.registerguard.
com/csp/cms/sites/web/
sports/25460937-41/oregon-
plays-kelly-offense-ducks.csp.

51 Sokolove, 5.

52 Wikipedia, "René Laennec,"
http://en.wikipedia.org/wiki/
Ren%C3%A9_Laennec#The_
invention_of_the_stethoscope.

53 Andrew Gumbel, "Viagra Rival
Cialis Boasts 40% Market
Share," *The Independent*,
March 24, 2004, http://
www.independent.co.uk/
news/business/news/
viagra-rival-cialis-boasts-40-
market-share-567443.html.

54 Stephen King, http://www.
stephenking.com/faq.html,
accessed June 15, 2009.

55 Matt Rosoff, "Bing Plus Yahoo
Now Equals Yahoo's Market
Share in 2005," businessinsider.
com, April 11, 2011, http://
www.businessinsider.com/
bing-tops-30-in-us-2011-4.

56 W. Chan Kim and Renee
Mauborgne, *Blue Ocean
Strategy: How to Create
Uncontested Market Space and
Make Competition Irrelevant*
(Boston: Harvard Business
School Publishing, 2005); Sun
Tzu, *The Art of War*, 9th ed.,
Ralph D. Sawyer, trans. (New
York: Basic Books, 1994); Al
Ries and Jack Trout, *Marketing
Warfare*, 2nd ed. (New York:
McGraw-Hill, 2005).

57 See, for example, Carl von
Clausewitz, *On War*, Michael
Howard and Peter Paret,
trans. and eds. (Princeton, NJ:
Princeton University Press,
1989).

58 The Bing Team, "Facebook
Friends Now Fueling Faster
Decisions on Bing," http://
www.bing.com/community/
site_blogs/b/search/
archive/2011/05/16/news-
announcement-may-17.aspx.

59 Malcolm Gladwell, *The Tipping
Point: How Little Things Can
Make a Big Difference* (Boston:
Little, Brown, 2000).

60 Sue Shellenbarger, "How to
Keep a Resolution," *Wall Street
Journal*, December 22, 2010,
D1-D2.

About the Author

Jim Link's fascination with ideas began as a child when he would invent new products in his head, then record commercials for his ideas on an old tape recorder he found in the basement. He eventually turned his love of new products and marketing into a career at General Mills, where he led new product efforts in the Snacks, Cereal, and Meals divisions.

Seeking to branch out into even more categories, Jim started his own idea company—Idea-Link, Inc.—at the age of thirty-three. Since 1994, Jim has helped over seventy organizations generate, refine, and market new ideas. Nearly all his clients are household names such as 3M, General Mills, Nestlé, Toro, Andersen Windows, Kohler, Marriott, Land O'Lakes, Heinz, Case-New Holland, and Cargill. His twenty-five years of new product and idea-generation work include experience in over 160 different product and service categories across four continents. Through it all, Jim has chosen to remain a one-man shop, focusing on doing the work he loves.

In addition to his consulting work, Jim is an engaging teacher who conducts training workshops on creativity, new products, and positioning, and he's a keynote speaker on these subjects at conferences. He is one of two outside instructors for 3M Marketing University, which reaches marketing, sales, and communication professionals across the globe. He also teaches creativity as a guest lecturer at major universities. He received his BA from Ohio Wesleyan University and his MBA in marketing from Michigan State University.

An avid but shockingly unproductive fisherman, Jim lives in Stillwater, Minnesota, with his wife, Janet, and their three children.